To Althea —

May the questions
on these pages lead
you into the lands
of answers that can
truly transform your
life.

Namasté
Wendy

What People Are Saying About
Ask Yourself *This*

A motivational book in its truest sense—it will get you moving. This book takes you by the hand and with its challenging and thought-provoking questions, gently but steadily pushes you along your path until you are ready to be "drawn forward by your brilliance."
—Hal Dunning, CEO and CFO, Barney & Barney LLC

Ask Yourself This offers vivid stories and vignettes that provide those seeking personal growth practical and understandable concepts to emulate. Exploration of every question can enhance your life through subtle yet significant changes in perspective. Anyone can practice these spiritual ideas, under any circumstances, in every moment, if one remains conscious and desires to transform their experience of life.
—Colonel Marianne Waldrop, United States Marine Corps

If you're looking for more meaning and joy in your life, *Ask Yourself This* is the guidebook for you. Wendy Craig-Purcell is a teacher's teacher who helps you tap into your personal wisdom, unlock your own answers, and create an authentic and purposeful life. Her book is entertaining, inspiring and thought-provoking and will transport you miles ahead on your spiritual path.
—Jan Phillips, Author/artist,
The Art of Original Thinking: The Making of a Thought Leader

I like this book! Wendy offers a sensitive and caring way to look at ourselves through asking important, practical questions that really count towards accelerating personal growth.

I especially liked the many interesting and inspirational stories used to paint a picture of each question asked. *Ask Yourself This* goes straight to the heart.

—Howard Martin, Coauthor,
The HeartMath Solution,
executive vice president, HeartMath LLC

There has rarely been a more exciting and important time to ask ourselves the questions in this powerful book. Deeply entering into these questions will do three things: it will open up new vistas on our sense of purpose; it will powerfully enrich our relationships with others; and it will bring even greater joy to our lives.

—Dr. Mark J. Weaver, Deep Storyworks

Once I started reading *Ask Yourself This*, I couldn't put it down. It is thought-provoking and easy to read, deep and illuminating, concise with absolutely no fluff. In a time of massive cultural change, of shattered beliefs, of security, and of impermanence, this book helps us to find a deeper security and encourages us to ask new and different questions, questions that we may have never asked ourselves, questions which may lead to different answers. Whether you are just beginning a path of inner exploration or are well on your way in your lifelong journey of transformation, you will find this book stimulating, revealing and uplifting. It is a must-read!

—Jeanne Anthony, Licensed clinical social worker

Bravo! Wendy reminds us that our best answers arise by asking our self the right *questions*. The practical suggestions, stories and humor bring lightness and fun to a deeply layered subject.

—Cynthia L. Henson, CEO, Henson Consulting Group

Ask Yourself This is a masterful guide to living the life you've always wanted, but didn't quite know how to create. Seamlessly blending practicality with idealism, clarity with depth and intelligence with heart, Craig-Purcell brings nearly 30 years of spiritual leadership and teaching excellence to her readers with refreshing immediacy and warmth. This book will sidle up next to you like an old friend and draw you into a dialogue that leaves you edified, clarified and utterly charmed. And when you put the book down and get back to the business of living your life, you'll carry with you a renewed sense of purpose and vision and the unshakable conviction that joy and fulfillment are already yours, hidden only by the fog of old, limiting ideas.

Employing a timeless Socratic method—asking powerful, transformative questions—Craig-Purcell creates a deeply engaging process that moves us out of listless (or worse) life patterns and onto an affirmative, vibrant life path that reveals the joy hidden within the ordinary moments of our extraordinary lives.

Thich Nhat Hanh said that "there is no way to peace. Peace is the way." Similarly, Craig-Purcell shows us that happiness is not a future achievement we must struggle to attain. Happiness is instead the now-experience of living fully in accord with our vision. In other words, happiness is not a goal—it is a by-product of a well-lived life. Like Aristotle, the Stoics, Buddha, Jesus and countless other wisdom teachers before her, Craig-Purcell shows us again that wisdom is within us, waiting only to be drawn out by the right questions. This is a book packed to the brim with just such questions. Read *Ask Yourself This* only if you are absolutely ready to begin living the life of your deepest, most daring dreams. There is no path to happiness. Happiness is the path. Let *Ask Yourself This* be a map.

—Peter Bolland, Professor of philosophy and humanities, Southwestern College, Chula Vista, California

Wendy Craig-Purcell

ASK *Yourself* THIS

Questions to open the heart,
expand the mind
and awaken the soul

unity®

HOUSE

Ask Yourself *This*
First edition 2009

To place an order, call the Customer Service department at 1-800-669-0282 or go online at *www.unity.org*.

Cover design by Karen Rizzo
Interior design by Karen Rizzo
Library of Congress Control Number: 2009926389
ISBN: 978-0-87159-336-8
Canada BN 13252 0933 RT

Dedication

*To Erna, my beloved grandmother, for being the one
to introduce me to Unity and for being the first person I
had the courage to talk to about becoming a minister.*

*To my parents, Bill and Lorraine Craig, for providing
me the loving foundation from which my life was launched.*

*To my son, Johnathon, without whose help
this book would still be only an idea.
And to my daughter, Jennifer—I love you more than life!*

*And most especially, to John, my husband and
life partner (the first and second time around), for quietly
believing in me and standing by me every step of the way
"for the long haul ... no matter what that looks like."*

Contents

Foreword

Wendy Craig-Purcell has the gift of making simple, direct and useful the great insights of humanity. In this book she offers us vital guidance in realizing our full potential self—how to connect our soul's destiny with the emerging world.

The essence of the message is that within each of us is an inner genius, the divine essence of the Life Force itself that is now pressing us to be more, to do more, to grow. No matter where we are in our journey, at whatever age or stage, this genius within is arising in all of us and calling us to a fuller expression. Because it is time!

We cannot grow spiritually in a dysfunctional world. We all can see that our civilization itself is in crisis. From an evolutionary perspective, these problems are "evolutionary drivers," awakening in us greater expression of our inner genius. Every one of us is a living member of a living planetary system undergoing its next phase of consciousness and growth. That means that each of us is being affected by this larger shift and needs guidance in fulfilling our own vocations of destiny in an evolving world. This book is one of our most valuable guides in exactly this moment of human history.

The key idea has been revealed over the ages. For me, it was through the critical observation of Dr. Abraham H. Maslow (founder of humanistic psychology) that all well, joyful, beneficent people had one trait in common: They had chosen work they find intrinsically self-rewarding and of service to at least one other person. In his great book *Toward a Psychology of Being*, Maslow described his decision to study well people rather than sick people. He mapped for us the characteristics of the self-actualizing person. He found that two of the most important factors in self-actualization are peak experiences: expanded reality, spiritual awakenings that set the field for our own emergence—and finding at least one other person who can recognize you, can see your essence and can call forth who you really are.

Wendy Craig-Purcell offers both of these gifts. Her spiritual understanding is for me a field of grace and resonance. And her ability to see who we truly are in our genius awakens that vocation of destiny and literally brings it forth! In my life experience, this inner calling expressed in creative action is the greatest gift we are given. It is God within. It always grows, always nourishes; it is ageless, beyond gender, beyond education. It is the divine essence within expressing itself.

This book aids us in affirming our evolutionary gifts, our genius, and connecting this creative essence with the emerging world. We can reread it as we would a poem or Scripture. It guides us in how to give our ongoing, emerging gift for the evolution of the self and the world.

Barbara Marx Hubbard,
Author, speaker and founder,
Foundation for Conscious Evolution

Introduction

By the usual standard of measurement—grades—I was considered a "smart kid" in school. I pulled straight A's just about every semester of high school. However, my grades—like those of many of my fellow classmates—were more a representation of how well I learned the right answers than how much I applied myself or how well I learned to think. For learning how to apply myself and think deeply, I have my father to thank. From his modeling, even more his direct instruction, I learned to value the thinking process itself and the importance of exercising my mind.

In a world where most of us still struggle for right answers, *Ask Yourself This* contends that the quality of our answers is directly related to the quality and timing of our questions. This is especially true as we seek to create lives that are personally fulfilling and help bring forth a world that can work for all.

> Quality questions create a quality life. Successful people ask better questions, and as a result, they get better answers.
> —Anthony Robbins, Author

French anthropologist Claude Levi-Strauss said, "The wise man doesn't give the right answers, he poses the right questions." Questions are like channels through which our mental, emotional and creative energy flows. Thus, the questions we ask greatly influence the quality of our lives. It behooves us, then, to make sure we are asking ourselves really good questions!

Ask Yourself This offers a variety of thought-provoking, perspective-shifting questions that can be applied in several key areas of life: spirituality, self-knowledge, personal growth, happiness and life purpose, relationships, inner genius and creativity, and success. The final chapter (especially for families) delves into some of the personal ways in which I have applied these questions within my own family.

> We learn more by looking for the answer to a question and not finding it than we do from learning the answer itself.
> —Lloyd Alexander, American novelist

> It is better to know some of the questions than all of the answers.
> —James Thurber, Author

Here are some suggestions on how to approach this material: First, be willing to sit with the questions. Let them simmer slowly and settle deeply. Resist the temptation to answer them too quickly or to assume there is only one "right" answer—after all, each answer will be uniquely your answer. Pick a few questions that really speak to you and memorize them. Let them serve as guides to deeper levels of yourself. Revisit them from time to time. These are questions to be lived with, not to be answered only once.

Second, I'd like to share tips gained by watching my 13-year-old daughter, Jennifer. As a minister and spiritual leader, I have been blessed to spend profound, quality time with some of the most inspiring people alive today: from world leaders such as His Holiness the Fourteenth Dalai Lama to great humanitarians such as Ela Gandhi (granddaughter of Mahatma Gandhi) and Dr. A.T. Ariyaratne (founder of the Sarvodaya movement). I've had the opportunity to meet many scientists, evolutionary biologists, futurists and best-selling authors and spiritual leaders. On many of these occasions, Jennifer has been present. I have watched her listening attentively to our conversations, trying to make sense of what was being said and not being afraid to ask questions when it was appropriate. I have admired the way she doesn't judge herself for not knowing. She is genuinely interested and curious. She remains engaged and doesn't withdraw, get frustrated, leave or compete. I sense her mind expanding as she grasps new information, and I am inspired to stretch my own thinking. Though she probably doesn't realize it, she is a role model for me, teaching me to listen more deeply, to stay engaged in conversations that stretch my understanding, to be patient with my own learning, and, most of all, to never fear asking good questions.

Isidor I. Rabi, a physicist and Nobel laureate recognized in 1944 for his discovery of nuclear magnetic resonance, was once asked by a friend how he became a scientist. He replied that every day after school his mother would ask him about his school day. She wasn't so much interested in what he had learned that day; she always wanted to know, "Did you ask a good question today?"

> You can tell whether a man is clever by his answers. You can tell whether he is wise by his questions.
> —Naguib Mahfouz, Author

"Asking good questions," Rabi said, "made me become a scientist."[1]

To which I would add: Asking good questions opens the door to personal transformation. I sincerely hope that after reading *Ask Yourself This*, you will have become a master at asking self-reflective questions that help you create the life you want and make the positive difference in the world that is yours to make.

Wendy Craig-Purcell

Chapter One

Ask Yourself *This*

To Grow Spiritually

Since I travel quite a bit, I often find myself on a crowded airplane holding conversations with strangers. The conversation usually begins with polite, safe questions: "Are you traveling home?" and "What do you do for a living?" I enjoy answering the first question, but not so much the second, as it often results in a moment of silent awkwardness.

When people hear that I am a minister, they usually respond in one of the following ways: They politely but quickly end the conversation—looking terrified that I might start talking about being "saved" (little do they know that in Unity we don't believe in "being saved" in the traditional Christian sense. We only believe in being saved from our own spiritual ignorance). Others feel guilty and obligated to explain why they don't like or attend church anymore. (After hearing some of their stories, I can't say I blame them!)

Then there are the bold ones, who seem to be looking for a debate or an opportunity to shock me. They will say, "Well, I don't believe in God anyway, so why bother with church?" (This is particularly ironic considering I've had so much difficulty with anything sounding or feeling "religious." When I was in ministerial school at Unity, I disliked using the word God so much—because of the popular image of God—that I gave "my" God a nickname. I called him "George." I have no idea why I picked George, it could have been Georgette, for that matter, since God is not anthropomorphic and is most definitely genderless.)

Anyway, to their comment "I don't believe in God," I will usually say, "Tell me about the God you don't believe in." I listen intently without comment. Invariably, the God they describe—a being residing in physical space and time (often looking like Michelangelo's God of the Sistine Chapel), meting out judgment, granting some wishes but not others, and rewarding those who believe in Him with everlasting salvation and punishing those who don't with eternal suffering—I simply smile and say "I don't believe in that God either."

> Religion is for those who don't want to go to Hell. Spirituality is for those of us who have already been through it.
>
> —Deepak Chopra,
> *The Path to Love*

My answer inevitably opens up a lively conversation in which we usually find some common ground as we begin to talk about an Ultimate Reality, a "higher presence," or an innate wisdom and intelligence operative in the universe.

Religion is a taboo subject for many people and irrelevant for many more. Spirituality, however, is an entirely different subject and one that is of growing interest throughout the world. According to George Gallup, internationally recognized researcher, "the pendulum may be swinging away from what is beyond to what is within us." A 1999 Gallup survey on American spirituality asked, "Do you think of spirituality more in a personal and individual sense or more in terms of organized religion and church doctrine?" Almost 75 percent of the respondents chose "personal and individual." In a January 2002 poll, 33 percent of Americans described themselves as "spiritual but not religious."[1]

Spirituality is not the same as religion, nor is it the same as morality.

How do you define spirituality? Is it a sense of a higher power? An energy or a presence greater than oneself? Some speak of it as innate intelligence and the organizing principle of the universe itself.

Religion, on the other hand, tends to rely on beliefs, rituals and doctrine to answer fundamental questions about the nature of man, the existence of good and evil, and God.

Morality deals with standards of conduct that are generally accepted as right or proper, whereas spirituality is concerned with the relationship between the individual and God or Spirit, Ultimate Truth, Atman, Buddha nature, or however you describe the Ineffable, Divine Presence. Ultimately, genuine spirituality is the communion, or nonseparate identification, with the innate and transcendent Divine Essence.

> Sometimes people get the mistaken notion that spirituality is a separate department of life, the penthouse of existence. But rightly understood it is a vital awareness that pervades all realms of our being.
> —Brother David Steindl-Rast, Benedictine Monk, Author, Spiritual Leader

Religion tends to divide us; spirituality tends to unite us. Religion tends to emphasize outer practice and conformation; spirituality emphasizes inner practice, personal transformation and the integration of higher levels of consciousness into day-to-day living.

While an undercurrent of spirituality runs throughout this book, this particular chapter poses specific questions to help you become more in touch with and expand your spirituality. These questions are intended to help you live a more contented, centered and rewarding (spiritual) life.

Ask Yourself This

What do I know for sure?

To grow spiritually, it is important to be clear on what you already know. The question "What do I know for sure?"

doesn't elicit your factual knowledge but rather what you know deep in the core of your being. It's the same distinction as that between knowing about God and knowing God. Knowing about God is theology; knowing God is spirituality.

> This is my simple religion. There is no need for temples; no need for complicated philosophy. Our own brain, our own heart is our temple; the philosophy is kindness.
> —His Holiness the Fourteenth Dalai Lama

Part of living a spiritual life is understanding what you know and believe and then living by those principles. It has nothing to do with adhering to religious doctrine. You can certainly do that if you choose, but living a spiritual life doesn't require adherence to a particular religion. Spirituality may include religious beliefs and practices, but it most definitely is not limited to them.

What do you know for sure? Not what have you been told to believe, but what do you truly believe? Asking this question provides a foundation for your life. Then you can add new insights that strengthen the core from which you live. Just as your childhood beliefs changed as you grew older, your current beliefs will likely evolve.

Here are some of the ideas that are central to my own beliefs:

• I know there is a power and presence (a "beingness," not a "being") that is everywhere equally present and is active in all of Life—and it is benevolent. It is transcendent and immanent; nearer to me than my own breath. It is the divine essence, the divine "stuff," out of which all that has taken form has come. It is the innate organizing principle of the Universe itself and is no respecter of persons. I live, move and have my being in it; and it lives, moves and finds expression through me. That which it is; I am. I am, indeed, made in its "image and likeness" (Gen. 2:26).

• I also know that everything happens for a reason and that ultimately everything unfolds for the highest and best. The operative word here is *ultimately*. We've all experienced situations which, at the time, felt like anything but good. We may have lost our job or gone through a divorce, been diagnosed with a serious illness, or experienced some other "dark night of the soul." Yet those very experiences—when met spiritually, consciously—can lead us to a much greater good. The lost job can be what finally motivates us to do whatever we need to do to discover the work that truly feeds our soul. The ending of a marriage can trigger us to do the emotional healing and personal growth work we've been avoiding for years. The challenge of disease can be what finally forces us to develop the habits and lifestyle changes needed for our health and well-being. Every one of us can look back at negative or painful experiences in our lives and say that while we are glad they're over, they turned out to be the "best worst things" that ever happened to us.

> When one door of happiness closes, another opens; but often we look so long at the closed door that we do not see the one which has been opened for us.
> —Helen Keller

Martha Smock, former editor of *Daily Word*, captured this realization in her poem "No Other Way."[2]

Could we but see the pattern of our days,
We should discern how devious were the ways
By which we came to this, the present time, this place in
    life;
And we should see the climb our soul has made up
    through the years.
We should forget the hurts, the wanderings, the fears,
    the wastelands of our life,
And know that we could come no other way or grow
    into our good

Without these steps our feet found hard to take, our faith
    found hard to meet.
The road of life winds on, and we like travelers go from
    turn to turn
Until we come to know the truth that life is endless
And that we forever are inhabitants of all eternity.

Though we may not see it in the moment, everything is
ultimately working for our greatest good—helping us evolve
into our highest and best selves.

• I also know the Greater Power and Presence I call *God*
is moving and evolving all the visible world into higher and
more complex expressions of good. When evidence of that
greater good is not readily apparent, I know that I am looking
through too narrow a window of time. If I look deeper, further
and wider, eventually, I will see it.

• Finally, I *know* that I co-create my life with Spirit. I
know that I am not a victim of fate, but rather the author of my
own life. I do not live by default, but by design. The choices I
make and the actions I take determine my future. I also know
that what I choose to focus on, I attract into my life. I am not
an innocent bystander of the story called "My Life." I am in
the driver's seat, and Spirit is riding shotgun.

What do *you* know for sure? What are the spiritual truths
that resonate in the very deepest part of your being?

Ask Yourself *This*
How big is my God?

Some people like to tell God how big their problems are;
others tell their problems how big their God is! The intent
behind the question "How big is my God?" is to deepen and
expand our belief in what's possible. It invites us to become

more aware of the wonder and miracle of the universe in which we live.

In a fascinating article called "Science Finds God," Sharon Begley writes:

> The more deeply scientists see into the secrets of the universe, you'd expect, the more God would fade away from their hearts and minds. But that's not how it went for Allan Sandage. He has spent a professional lifetime coaxing secrets out of the stars, peering through telescopes in the hope of spying nothing less than the origins and destiny of the universe. He has actually figured out how fast the universe is expanding and how old it is (15 billion years or so) through his observations of distant stars. But through it all, he who says he was "almost a practicing atheist as a boy," was nagged by the mysteries whose answers were not to be found in the glittering panoply of supernovas. Among them: Why is there something rather than nothing? He began to despair of answering such questions through reason alone, and so at 50, he willed himself to accept God. "It was my science that drove me to the conclusion that the world is much more complicated than can be explained by science. It is only through the supernatural that I can understand the mystery of existence.[3]

> I find it quite improbable that such order came out of chaos. There has to be some organizing principle. God to me is a mystery but is the explanation for the miracle of existence, why there is something instead of nothing.
> —Allan Sandage,
> Winner of the
> Crawfoord prize in astronomy

> The exquisite order displayed by our scientific understanding of the physical world calls for the divine.
> —Vera Kistiakowsky,
> MIT physicist

Whether it's through examining more deeply the mysteries of the universe, personally meditating on "why there is something rather than nothing" or being inspired by true stories of the miraculous and unexplainable, every one of us can catapult our spiritual growth by reexamining and expanding our concept of God.

I define miracles as the result of a perfect alignment between humans and the power of Spirit within. The founding of the Unity movement is the result of a miraculous physical healing.

Unity was founded in the late 1800s by Charles (1854–1948) and Myrtle (1845–1931) Fillmore. Neither had intended to start what would become a worldwide spiritual movement.

As a child, Myrtle was diagnosed with tuberculosis. At that time, a cure for tuberculosis did not exist. So she spent her childhood and much of her adult life with a vibrant spirit trapped in a sickly body, believing there was nothing she could do about her condition.

When Myrtle was in her thirties, she met and married Charles Fillmore. Charles also had physical challenges. When he was a boy, he seriously injured his hip in an ice skating accident that stunted the growth in his right leg. To walk, he needed a brace and an elevated shoe; even with those, he walked with a noticeable limp.

When Myrtle was 41, she became very ill from the tuberculosis and was given six months to live. As a young woman, wife and mother, she was strongly motivated to find a cure. While she and Charles attended a class in Chicago taught by metaphysician Dr. Eugene B. Weeks, she heard a statement that was in direct opposition to how she had been taught to think about herself. The statement resonated deep in her soul: "I am a child of God, and therefore I do not inherit sickness." She began to work with this new idea, affirming it on a daily basis. She spoke healing words to every cell in her body. And, within two years, she was completely healed (and lived to be 86!).

Family and friends who witnessed her healing were naturally curious and began to ask her questions. She shared her practice of affirmative prayer, and they started praying too, and benefiting from the practice. Charles' prayer work eventually resulted in a lengthening of his leg to such an extent that he was able to discard his leg brace and shoe lift and walk with a barely noticeable limp.

Charles and Myrtle continued studying world religions and philosophies and the link between religion and science. They began writing about their own discoveries and beliefs. Shortly thereafter, the Unity movement was born.

What a powerful story from which we can learn so much! Clearly Myrtle's concept of God grew over time. She realized that the God of her being—her inner divinity—was greater than her illness. She was able to heal herself because she dramatically changed her perception of what was possible with God. She told her problem how big her God was.

If we limit our perception of God, we limit what we are able to accomplish. Through spiritual practice, we can overcome many obstacles but only if we hold the space for an infinitely powerful God within us.

Ask Yourself This

How wide is my circle? (How open am I?)

He drew a circle that shut me out;
    heretic, rebel, a thing to flout.
        But love and I had the wit to win.
            We drew a circle that took him in."
—Edwin Markham, from his poem "Outwitted"[4]

The question "How wide is my circle?" helps us get in touch with who and what we shut out. Growing spiritually involves being genuinely open to more people, possibilities and experiences. If we are closed to the divine impulse, then our ability to expand as spiritual beings and embrace others with love is greatly diminished. We lose not only the ability to grow but also the ability to function as our best selves. If we limit ourselves in any way, we restrict the expression of God through us.

How are you limiting yourself? How are you holding yourself back? In a world all too eager to place limits and restrictions on you, why put any more limits on yourself? How are you shutting out other people and possibilities?

Probing this question lets us examine how we can expand our thinking and being. Spirituality is inclusive by nature. To grow spiritually, we must become more inclusive. Respecting our fellow human beings despite our differences creates a more peaceful and joyous world. Opening our hearts to include others brings happiness to all.

> Life must be lived on a higher plane. We must go up to a higher platform, to which we are always invited to ascend; there, the whole aspect of things changes.
> —Ralph Waldo Emerson

> I don't like that man.
> I must get to know him better.
> —Abraham Lincoln

> I like your Christ; I do not like your Christians. You Christians are so unlike your Christ.
> —Mohandas Gandhi

There is a story that during World War I, a Protestant chaplain was assigned to the American troops in Italy. While there, he became close friends with the local priest. Later, the chaplain and his troops were relocated, and soon afterwards the chaplain was killed.

Upon hearing of his friend's death, the priest petitioned the military and requested that the chaplain be buried in his parish cemetery, explaining that they had been close friends. Since the chaplain had no other family, the request was granted. But when the priest asked permission from the Catholic Church, it was denied because the chaplain was not Catholic. Disappointed, the priest, not wanting to risk losing his parish yet wanting his friend's grave close by, buried the chaplain just outside the cemetery's fence.

A few years later one of the chaplain's troop members returned. Wanting to pay his respects to the chaplain, he asked the priest if he could see the gravesite.

The priest led the man to the place where the chaplain had been buried, and the man was astonished to see that the chaplain's grave lay within the cemetery's fence. Amazed and elated, he said, "I don't believe it! I see you finally got permission to bury the chaplain in the cemetery."

"No, not exactly," the priest smiled. "They told me where I couldn't bury the body, but they never said I couldn't move the fence."

We all have places where we need to "move our fences" and open our hearts to receive and give more. Who or what are you shutting out? Are those whose skin color is different than yours included in your circle? How about those whose sexual orientation is different from yours? Or those whose political persuasions are at the opposite end of the spectrum?

We need to draw our circle wider to take in the beauty of the world beyond. Perhaps then we can do more than simply *move* the fence and instead *remove* it and embrace the wholeness of the human family.

Ask Yourself *This*

How much room do I give God to work it out?

When our spiritual community outgrew the place we were leasing, it became apparent that we needed to move. So we began looking for a larger building to purchase near our existing location. The search proved very difficult and time-consuming because of the parking requirements for the thousand-seat sanctuary we had planned. Eventually, we did find a building—14 miles from the existing one—that seemed perfect. It was right off the freeway on a lovely piece of property surrounded by lush eucalyptus trees. We made an offer. We got no response. Our agent kept following up. No response. I kept praying and visualizing every day, convinced this was the perfect right place for us. Despite numerous phone calls and letters we never got a response. (Our real estate agent eventually learned that the owner was holding out for a full cash offer expected to come.)

It was not until I finally let go that our agent found another building for sale that met our requirements even better, and this owner eagerly returned our calls and responded to our offer. We bought the building. It has been the location of our spiritual center now for almost 17 years, providing us with a beautiful location for our work. (Interesting, the other building remained empty for years and was purchased only a year ago!)

> Everything I ever let go of has claw marks on it.
> —Anne Lamott, Author
>
> We must let go of the life that we have planned, so as to accept the one that is waiting for us.
> —Joseph Campbell, Author

"Letting go" is a powerful way of giving God some room to work it out.

When people first begin a spiritual practice such as affirmative prayer and visualization, they often exercise a great deal of determined will to try to control the outcome. They become convinced that their prayer should be answered in a specific way and seem totally unwilling to give the Innate Intelligence of the Universe any leeway to work it out. But part of growing spiritually is being able to hold the seeming paradox of praying for and visualizing what you desire while at the same time being willing for that or something different and better to emerge. If we are holding on so tightly to just one possibility, we will miss seeing the other possibilities that may be even better. When we step back and give Spirit room to work through us, not only does our spirituality grow exponentially, but we also discover greater peace of mind because we have finally let go of what we were trying to control.

Ask Yourself *This*

Is faith or fear guiding my decisions?

One of the most profound ways of living a more spiritual life is to examine the motivation behind our actions. For many of us, our primary motivator is fear. While fear certainly encourages action, it does not encourage *conscious* action. Fear promotes impulsive decisions. Faith, on the other hand, results in decisions made from a higher state of consciousness after deep thought. Fear encourages us to be afraid, while faith encourages us to be affirmative. Sometimes we feel stuck, believing we need more faith to get started. But in truth, we already have the faith we need within us. We must simply call it forth. Faith grows and expands with use. As it grows, it pushes fear aside, making the seemingly impossible become possible.

This illustration is one of my all-time favorites for reminding me that a little faith exercised at the beginning can be strengthened along the way to accomplish amazing feats.

> He has not learned the first lesson of life who does not every day surmount a fear.
> —Ralph Waldo Emerson

In 1847 the first suspension bridge to span the Niagara River was commissioned. The bridge was to connect the Canadian side of the river with the American side. In that day and age, the usual method for getting the first cable across the river would have been to drag it across by boat. However, because of the site's proximity to Niagara Falls, the currents were so strong that stretching the first cable by boat was not an option. It occurred to one of the engineers, however, that if a kite could be flown across the gorge, the kite's string could be used as the first line on which subsequent cords and then cables could be drawn across. A contest was held to see if someone could successfully fly a kite across the 800-foot-wide river and win the five dollars in prize money. After a lot of hard work and several failed attempts, a 10-year-old boy named Homan Walsh successfully flew his kite across the river. The string of his kite was then fastened to a tree and used to draw a light cord across. Heavier cord followed until finally a wire cable spanned the gap, which became the foundational cable of the new bridge.[5]

Thin as that kite string was in comparison to the cables and eventually the bridge that spanned the river, it was enough!

Trust in the faith that you *do* have. Use it and build on it, rather than worrying about how much more you wish you had.

What is driving your decisions today? Are you spurned by fear or drawn by faith? Stop and ask yourself, "If faith were guiding my decision, what would I do?" Sometimes your faith may feel like a kite string and your fear like a wide and raging river, but you reach a place of greater spiritual understanding when you have the courage to allow that strand of faith to weave your future. The more we rely on faith, the stronger our faith becomes.

Ask Yourself *This*

What am I listening for and to?

Here's a tale of two colleagues who were walking down a busy Manhattan street during their lunch break. One was raised in New York City, and the other grew up on a Native American reservation. As they were walking through the crowds with the smog clogging their nostrils and the horns pounding against their eardrums, the Native American stopped and said, "Wait a minute! I think I heard something!"

The native New Yorker stopped with a look of bewilderment and asked, "What did you hear? The traffic?"

"No," the Native American colleague replied, "I heard a cricket."

"You heard a cricket?" his friend asked incredulously. "You couldn't possibly hear a cricket in the midst of all of this noise."

"No. I heard a cricket."

He crossed the street and walked to a planter box there. Sure enough, pushing aside a leaf, he revealed the cricket.

Astounded, the native New Yorker exclaimed, "You're amazing. You have superhuman hearing. How could you hear that cricket above all of this noise?"

His colleague replied, "I don't have superhuman hearing. It just depends on what you choose to listen for. Everyone else has the same ability. I'll prove it to you." Taking out a handful of coins, the Native American dropped them on the busy

> The next message you need is always right where you are.
> —Ram Dass

> Do not assume that divine guidance flows only when you are in need of help. Guidance continues to flow whether or not you have problems.
> —Caroline Myss,
> *Entering the Castle*

New York sidewalk. For about 10 feet all around them, everyone stopped to look for the source of the noise, wondering if they had dropped their keys, their wallet or some money.

What are you listening *for* and what are you listening *to*? Spiritual growth can be enhanced by listening for that still small voice of higher guidance within. If you take time to become quiet and listen attentively, you will notice wisdom within you that has the ability to lead you on your journey through life. Listening *for* that voice is not enough, however. If you fail to listen *to* it, then you have only accomplished half your goal.

Too often we listen for the voice of guidance, but when it calls us to do something we don't know how to do or are afraid to do, we turn a deaf ear to it. We hope we've been contacted by mistake and that the message we heard was really for someone else! There are no accidents. The voice of higher guidance that speaks to you, speaks only to you. Listen *for* it and *to* it, and your life will change for the better.

Ask Yourself *This*

What is God preparing me for?

We are all here by divine appointment. We all have a divine purpose we are meant to fulfill. One of the ultimate goals of spiritual growth is to identify the nature of our purpose and then to live it. This is not fate. It is not destiny. This is the finding and fulfilling of one's divine assignment. Regardless of what you are doing now, you are capable of doing more. The universe is preparing you to fulfill the purpose that you and only you can complete. There is something greater that you are called to do. I can't tell you what it is; only the voice inside can tell you; but you have to be open, and you have to be paying attention.

Sometimes all it takes is one moment of understanding for our purpose to be revealed.

I personally know how powerful and fulfilling it is to find—and live—one's purpose. From a very young age, I knew that I was here to make a significant and positive difference in the world. Perhaps every idealistic youth feels that way. Like others my age, in my junior and senior years of high school I spent considerable time thinking about what my major would be in college. I thought about all the helping professions I was familiar with. Should I pursue a career in medicine and become a doctor? Should I study the inner workings of the psyche and become a psychologist? What about teaching or social work? For various reasons, none of those seemed quite right. Intuitively I knew I wanted to work with the whole person. Medicine, at that time, still largely approached healing from a purely physical point of view excluding the importance of the mental, emotional and spiritual aspects of one's being. Psychology and teaching focused on the mental levels and social work was often constrained by the bureaucratic systems within which it had to function. I wanted to work with the whole of a person's being: spirit, mind, heart and soul. Though I had by no means decided on my major, I studied hard and made sure I got the best grades I could.

Two life-altering events happened during my last year of high school. I was introduced to Unity by my grandmother, and my years devoted to figure skating resulted in my being offered a contract to skate professionally with Ice Capades when I graduated. I pursued the skating; but not Unity. While all my friends were preparing to go away to college, I was packing a steamer trunk filled with my skates and costumes and heading for Duluth, Minnesota, for training. I was just 17 at the time and had never been away from home. I didn't last long. Though I loved skating, in less than a week's time, I knew I was not in my right place. I could not be a showgirl. I broke my contract and came home feeling quite lost and very embarrassed. By then it was clear my skating days were over, and it was too late to enter college that semester.

So I decided to go to work for the remainder of the school year, take a few courses at the local community college to try to identify my major, and eventually enroll in the university. I met someone and fell madly in love. In a rather short time, I realized the relationship could go nowhere. My heart was broken, and I needed some help. I remembered my few visits to Unity and the practical, spiritual ideas I had heard expressed there. I decided to check it out again.

Every Sunday I heard something I could apply that week. Practical, spiritual wisdom. I often felt the minister was talking just to me. I devoured the Unity books and read *Daily Word* magazine every morning. After several months, my broken heart had healed and I was filled with joy and optimism about my future. I enjoyed my job and was still considering what I would major in in college. But something very strange started to happen. I would be sitting in church and all of a sudden my mind would flash and I would "see" myself on the platform speaking. That image and thought was very disturbing to me. It was frightening. Ministers were men—older men—and I was a young woman barely 20 years old. Ministers were religious; I definitely was not. Ministers were outgoing, and I'm an introvert. Ministers were comfortable speaking in front of large groups of people every week, and I most definitely was not. (The only class I ever dropped out of was Speech, when I was told that the following week I'd have to stand before my classmates and give a two-minute talk about myself, and I was terrified at that thought.) This vision had to be wrong! I couldn't possibly be destined to go into the ministry. Not me.

I was successful in suppressing the premonition for awhile, but then it started to show up in my dreams and I would awaken from the image frightened and annoyed. When the dreams wouldn't stop, I decided I needed to do something. I needed to talk to someone I could trust. I was too embarrassed to share such nonsense with my parents, so I decided to talk to my grandmother, figuring that since she had introduced me to Unity, she would be able to make sense of it and she would set me straight.

I gave her a call and told her I needed her wise counsel. She invited me over for dinner. All through dinner I hemmed and hawed about bringing up the subject. Finally, just when I got up the courage to open the subject, she told me to wait. She said she needed to get something first. She left the room for a few minutes and when she came back, she handed me a sealed envelope. In it was a note she had written to me months before telling me of *her* premonition that I was being called into ministry. In that moment I knew I was being called into my life's purpose and that I was being prepared for the work I was to do—work that has allowed me for nearly three decades now to make a positive difference in people's lives spiritually, mentally and emotionally.

> I learned this, at least, by my experiment: that if one advances confidently in the direction of his dreams, and endeavors to live the life which he had imagined, he will meet with a success unexpected in common hours.
> —Henry David Thoreau

> Destiny grants us our wishes, but in its own way, in order to give us something beyond our wishes.
> —Johann Wolfgang von Goethe, Poet

God has something for you to do, too, and if you pay attention to the clues (and keep asking good questions), you will find out what that something is!

Chapter Two

Ask Yourself *This*

To Know Yourself Better

Our deepest fear is not that we are inadequate. Our deepest fear is that we are powerful beyond measure. It is our light, not our darkness, that most frightens us. We ask ourselves, Who am I to be brilliant, gorgeous, talented, fabulous? Actually, who are you not to be? You are a child of God. Your playing small does not serve the world. There is nothing enlightened about shrinking so that other people won't feel insecure around you. We were born to make manifest the glory of God that is within us. It's not just in some of us; it's in everyone. And as we let our own light shine, we unconsciously give other people permission to do the same. As we are liberated from our own fear, our presence automatically liberates others.

—Marianne Williamson, *A Return to Love*[1]

> Knowing others is intelligence; knowing yourself is true wisdom. Mastering others is strength; mastering yourself is true power.
> —Lao Tse, *Tao Te Ching*
>
> Your vision will become clear only when you look into your heart. Who looks outside, dreams. Who looks inside, awakens.
> —Carl Jung, Psychologist

How do you view yourself? Do you focus on your light, or do you dwell on your shadow? Are you even aware of everything that characterizes who you are? These are different ways of asking "How well do you know yourself?" Stop and think. How well do you really know yourself? How much time have you spent exploring what lies within you? Plato counseled, "Know thyself above all else." Conscious awareness of who we are is the foundation of a happy and whole life.

Many times we are frightened by what we find when we look within. Our carefully constructed images of ourselves may prove false. The labels we have used to describe ourselves may not be accurate. We may even confront aspects of ourselves that we dislike.

True, unwavering self-love comes from knowing and embracing all parts of ourselves. We cannot deny the qualities we consider less than perfect. Our darkness is just as much a part of us as our light. Author and spiritual leader Deepak Chopra has said, "If you do not see your shadow, it is because you are standing in the dark." In fact, seeing our shadow is necessary for truly appreciating our divinity. Just as we see the brilliant stars best on the darkest nights, so, too, do we realize and appreciate our own light when viewed against the backdrop of our humanness.

The questions on the following pages are meant to help you deeply explore all parts of your being so that you can begin to fall in love with yourself. Once you rediscover yourself on your deepest level, you can begin to truly evolve into a higher, more authentic and loving expression of you.

The final frontier is not outer space but inner space. Ask these questions with a childlike curiosity and sense of discovery. Pretend you are meeting yourself for the first time. Take time to get to know yourself.

Ask Yourself *This*

Who do I think I am?

Don't ask this question from the usual place of doubt and insecurity. Ask this question to explore your own perceptions of yourself. This is seemingly one of the simplest self-discovery questions, but it requires deep reflection. What do you think of yourself? Who do you think you are? We are all more complex and wondrous than we believe. The spark of the divine and the innate potential within each of us is more vast than we could possibly imagine. Our internal power is always there waiting to be expressed. We need only say "yes" to it.

> What a man thinks of himself, that is what determines, or rather indicates, his fate.
> —Henry David Thoreau

> I always wanted to be somebody, but now I realize I should have been more specific.
> —Lily Tomlin

My friend Mary went on a family vacation with her daughter and son-in-law to Mexico. While Mary's picture of an ideal vacation was to relax while reading inspirational books, her daughter and son-in-law had something else in mind. After teasing and cajoling her, they convinced Mary to try driving an all-terrain vehicle in the sand dunes. As her daughter and son-in-law zipped past her in glee, Mary crept along, white knuckles gripping the handlebars. When she saw what fun the kids were having and how much faster they were going, she wondered if there was something wrong with her vehicle. Seeing her struggle, her son-in-law pulled up and whispered in her ear, "Mama, you have power you're not using. Take your foot off the brake."

Like Mary, we all have power we're not using. But if we're riding the brake, we can't access it. Do you realize that you have tremendous power within and that you need only take your foot off the brake to let it flow through you? Or do you think you are incapable of living bigger? Who *do* you think you are? You have power within you that has been untapped and overlooked. Let go of your past limited views of yourself and you can release this vast potential.

We have all become so adept at categorizing ourselves that we forget that labels are nothing more than human attempts to classify and organize. A label is not the thing itself. It is both possible and exciting to venture out beyond the limits of the labels we've assumed. Many people derive their own sense of identity from the way others describe them. But our true identity is independent of external judgments. Our true identity comes from within. We must not allow ourselves to be held back by anyone else's perceptions. What we've accepted about ourselves in the past does not have to control who we will become in the future. We can make other choices!

Take time to explore who you think you are. Realize, though, that no matter how well you may think you know yourself, you are always changing. Thus your understanding of yourself must also change.

Our inner consciousness is the final frontier because, regardless of any current certainty or understanding, our ever-evolving nature eludes permanent classification. Explore who you think you are and then let go of that limiting image. You are far greater than you can even imagine.

> People travel to wonder at the height of mountains, at the huge waves of the sea, at the long courses of rivers, at the vast compass of the ocean, at the circular motion of the stars; and they pass by themselves without wondering.
>
> —St. Augustine

> If those who lead you say to you, "See, the kingdom is in the sky," then the birds of the sky will precede you. If they say to you, "It is in the sea," then the fish will precede you. Rather, the kingdom is inside you, and it is outside of you. When you come to know yourselves, then you will become known, and you will realize that it is you who are the sons of the living Father. But if you will not know yourselves, you will dwell in poverty and it is you who are that poverty.
>
> —From the Gospel of Thomas

Ask Yourself *This*

What do I say "yes" to in my life?

Examining what we say "yes" to or what we agree to in our lives can tell us a lot about our priorities. Priorities can, in turn, tell us a great deal about ourselves. Where we spend our time and money is a powerful indicator of what we truly value. If you open your calendar, your checkbook and your credit card statement, you will see an important picture of what you are saying "yes" to in your life. We vote with how we spend our

> Actions express priorities.
> —Mohandas Gandhi
>
> We do not have a money problem in America. We have a values and priorities problem.
> —Marian Wright Edelman,
> Activist

dollars and how we spend our time. What do you agree to in your life? Through both your words and actions, what do you say "yes" to?

A fun exercise is to ask yourself the following questions to see how you show up while doing life's routine tasks. The answers are valuable indicators of what you consciously or unconsciously project to the world.

How do you drive in traffic? Our habits when behind the wheel speak volumes. When faced with a sea of brake lights ahead, do you aggressively change lanes to find the fastest route? Or do you calmly wait for your turn to move? When the light turns yellow, do you step on the gas even though you could stop? Or do you steadily but firmly apply the brakes so as not to risk an accident?

When you play board games with your family or friends, do you play for the sheer fun of it or do you play only to win?

How do you talk to your mother when you think no one is listening? Do you treat those close to you with love because you want to? Or because you feel you have to?

How do you treat your waiter or waitress at a restaurant? We can determine a lot about how we perceive our own status from how we treat those who serve us.

What do you spend your money on? Where we place our hard-earned income is one of the most powerful assessments of our priorities.

What makes you laugh? Humor can reveal our inner nature. Do you laugh at the expense of others? Or do you laugh with the joy and elation of others?

What makes you angry? What makes you cry? The way you respond to annoyances, challenges and hardships provides a snapshot of the inner workings of your personality.

We can learn even more about our inner selves by examining any discrepancies between what we value and what we are projecting through our actions. When we can identify differences in what we believe and how we actually show up in life, we can begin to see how our life is a manifestation of our consciousness. What are we really saying "yes" to in our day-to-day actions?

If there is a discrepancy between how we live and what we believe in, our lives will lack coherence. We feel it when we are not living according to our highest, most closely held values. We feel unfulfilled and scattered. While living according to our values isn't easy, addressing the discrepancies is the first step to living a more authentic life and truly loving ourselves.

Ask Yourself *This*

What am I looking for?

There is a story I've heard about twin brothers who, though nearly identical in appearance, were completely different in their ways of being. One saw everything in life as a miracle. Even at a young age he looked for the good in everything and always experienced life as positive. His twin, on the other hand, always found something wrong with even the happiest circumstances and most perfect of days. He was pessimistic and rather miserable because he rarely found anything positive in life.

Concerned about the extremes in their sons' behaviors, the twins' parents sought help from a counselor.

After hearing the parents' description of their children, the counselor devised a test to assess the degree of their optimistic or pessimistic tendencies. The pessimistic child was placed in a room filled with every toy imaginable. However, all he did was complain about the lack of friends to play with. The optimistic child, on the other hand, was placed in another room that was full of manure. Through the two-way mirrors, the parents and counselor saw the child on his hands and knees digging through the manure. Shocked and very concerned, the counselor entered the room and asked what the boy was doing. The child replied, "With all this manure, there's got to be a pony in here somewhere!"

> People only see what they are prepared to see.
> —Ralph Waldo Emerson
>
> The way we see the problem, is the problem.
> —Stephen Covey,
> *The Seven Habits of Highly Effective People*

"What are you looking for?" is another way of asking, "Where do you place your attention?" Our focus influences our experiences. If we emphasize life's beauty and wonder, we will experience more of life's gifts. However, if we focus only on problems and challenges, soon that becomes the only thing we notice. This negativity then perpetuates in a destructive cycle of pessimistic energy.

So where should we place our focus? What should we look for? As with the earlier question, "What do I say yes to?" this question helps us identify to where we are directing our time and energy. Then if we want to make a change, we can re-direct our time and energy into something we want to grow.

Ask Yourself *This*

Do I live by one set of rules?

This is where we often begin to discover the parts of our-selves that we don't like and have tried to hide for so long. This question, along with the next one, is meant to gently reveal portions of your shadow so that you can see yourself in your entirety and then embrace who you are as a whole. Do not approach this process from a place of guilt. Most likely, it is that very guilt that caused you to bury these portions of your identity in the first place. The goal is to remove the fear of rediscovering them and then to begin to heal and love the parts of you that you have made wrong.

Do you live by one set of rules? Do you have just one standard by which you live? Obviously we are more relaxed and at ease around family and friends than at a formal gathering, but do we change our conduct drastically based on our environment? If you are a parent, do you act differently when you know your children are watching? If you are in a committed relationship, do you behave differently when your partner is around? Are there things that you do privately that you know are not a reflection of your highest values or beliefs, but you do them anyway? Another way of putting it is, "If I was doing business with God, would I need to change any of my practices?"

> Have the courage to say no. Have the courage to face the truth. Do the right thing because it is right. These are the magic keys to living your life with integrity.
> —W. Clement Stone, Businessman

We bend the rules in many ways. For example, despite

the fact that the speed limit on most of our freeways is 65 miles per hour, most people drive at 70 miles per hour or more. Then when we see a highway patrolman, we immediately slow down to a legal speed. We're using two sets of rules here.

While this is a minor example, it illustrates how, when we live by drastically different rules, we lose sight of who we are. If we feel we have to put on a façade for the rest of the world, we often become so accustomed to that image of ourselves that we forget it is a false portrayal of who we really are.

Story has it, when actor Robert Redford was at the height of his career, he encountered an adoring fan in an elevator. After staring at him for some time, the woman asked breathlessly, "Are you the real Robert Redford?"

Slowly he replied, "Only when I am alone, ma'am."

The price we pay for living by double standards is a loss of authenticity and free expression. Whether we hide the actions we consider inappropriate or simply do not express our true selves, we make a portion of ourselves wrong and fail to love ourselves fully.

Ask Yourself *This*

Where do I distort the truth?

A story in *Reader's Digest* told of a father and his daughter, who were eating at a steakhouse. The father ordered his favorite T-bone as he always did because he loved to take the bone home to chew on. When they finished their meal, the father asked the waitress to put the bone in a takeout bag for his dog. When the waitress left, his daughter says, "But Dad, we don't *have* a dog."

"I know," he admitted "but it's too embarrassing to admit I want it for myself."

The waitress returned a few minutes later holding a very large bag. "Here, I wanted to make sure you had plenty of bones for your dog," she explained, "so I went through the scrap bucket and grabbed all the T-bones I could find."

Sometimes we distort the truth in larger and more serious ways. But instead of punishing ourselves for the times we are less than honest, we can use them to learn more about ourselves. This father might probe a little deeper and ask, "Why did I feel the need to compromise my honesty?" If we can pinpoint where and why we bend the truth and understand how doing so undermines who we really are, we will be more likely to make better choices in the future.

Our children often show us where we are less than totally honest or where we are not "walking our talk." They zero in on any inconsistency as if they had radar. They notice whether our words and actions are congruent.

I remember taking my son, Johnathon, to the movies one day. It was right after he had turned 12 and had to start paying the adult price. When the cashier asked how many tickets I needed, I said, "Two adults."

Looking at Johnathon, she asked how old he was. I told her that he had just turned 12. "Oh," she said as she handed me our tickets, "You could have just told me he was 11 and I wouldn't have known the difference."

"Yes, but he would have known, and so would I."

Being a good example for my son and maintaining my own integrity was far more important to me than saving a few dollars.

Ask Yourself *This*

What in me is allowing this to continue?

Life does not happen to us, it happens *through* us. You are a co-creator of your life with Spirit. While this is no doubt empowering, it can also be challenging because it prevents us from being able to blame our problems on someone else.

The truth is that you are responsible for where you are in your life. That can be both energizing and challenging because it requires you to take responsibility for the negative things in your life as well as the positive. Most of us find it far easier to play the victim. Living consciously and co-creatively takes daily practice, discipline and effort. Self-discovery is not simply accomplished by going to church, reading a book, attending a seminar or sitting at the feet of an enlightened master.

Examining "What in me is allowing this to continue?" moves us out of victimhood, where life seems to be happening to us, and moves us to a place of empowerment, where we are directing our own life. Our responsibility goes far beyond simply assuring our physical and mental well-being. It means realizing that, whether consciously or not, we have helped create the life we are living. This can be overwhelming if we find ourselves faced with serious challenges; but it can also be empowering when we realize we can use this same co-creative process to bring forth something new and better.

The following story illustrates how we create the life we live.

A skilled carpenter worked for many years for a general contractor building beautiful homes. When he turned 65, he decided it was time to retire. The general contractor was very fond of him and was sad to see him go. As a personal favor, the general contractor asked if he would build him one last house. It was to be a very special house made of the finest materials and craftsmanship. And, because it was the last house the carpenter was to build, he was invited to put a good profit margin in it for himself.

The carpenter agreed but it soon became apparent that his heart was no longer in his work. He cut corners, compromised excellence, and did not put forth the same quality of work he was known for. Hurriedly, he finished the house and informed his boss. They met at the house for the final walk-through. When the contractor opened the door for the inspection, he paused, turned to the carpenter and handed him the keys saying, "You have done such good work for me over the years. In appreciation for all you've done for me, this is my farewell gift to you. You built this house for yourself."

Events, circumstances ... have their origin in our selves. They spring from seeds which we have sown.
—Henry David Thoreau

What you are comes to you.
—Ralph Waldo Emerson

What within you allows the undesirable aspects of your life to continue? It doesn't have to be that way. You have the ability to change your life. The first step is realizing that you have that power within you, then determining what you want to change. You don't have to wait for anyone but yourself. Make it a priority to discover who you are. You will find you are far greater than you ever imagined and *you* have the power to make your life even greater.

Of all the investments you can make, the investment in personal growth and development is by far the most important. The quality of your word, the soundness of your promise, your follow-through on delivery, doing what you say you are going to do, and your trustworthiness are critically important. It isn't always easy or expedient to do the right thing or to stay in integrity. Nor is it always the most popular. But it is vitally important. Every time you act with integrity, a part of your divinity is amped up. Your consciousness expands and your goodness flows into the world. Getting to know yourself more fully and honestly is not a task for the faint of heart or the impatient. There are no shortcuts to personal transformation. But the rewards are in living the life and being the person you've always dreamed of.

Chapter Three

Ask Yourself *This*

To Grow Personally

In the last chapter we explored "Who are you now?" Now we will ask, "Who would you like to be?" It is not a problem if there are differences in your answers to these two questions. In fact, it signals one of the most powerful opportunities we have as human beings: the chance for personal growth. Where the human species is now is the result of continual evolution and adaptation; similarly, where you are now as an individual is the product of your physical and psychological growth from infancy to adulthood. You were not always the "you" you are today. You grew into the person, the body, the mind and the consciousness you now are.

Much of this growth is automatic. As children, we don't consciously develop our understanding of the world; our experiences provide us with all the data our budding brains need. We reach an age, however, when the effects of hormones, new social experiences and our natural development slows down. It is from this place that we begin to explore who we are and come to know ourselves. Once we know ourselves well, we can make conscious and informed choices to change and grow.

How would you like to grow personally? Who is it that you want to become? How do you want to "be"? The very personal nature of these questions precludes any single path for everyone. Use the questions in this chapter to stimulate other questions that can guide you on your individual path of personal growth.

Ask Yourself *This*

What is my intention?

As a teenager, I was a dedicated ice skater. Every morning at 4 a.m., I would wake up and go to the rink before school. After years of hard work, private lessons and lots of practice, my skating became good enough that I was given the opportunity to skate as a professional with the Ice Capades. Even more than competing as an amateur or skating in a show, I enjoyed skating up to a child who was trying the sport for the first time and offering to give them a few pointers. After convincing them to let go of the rail and take my hand, we would begin to skate around the perimeter of the rink. Most did fine until they came to the end of the straightaway and we needed to turn. They would often stiffen up and stop. The secret, though, was to keep moving and to look in the direction they wanted to go. If they focused their attention and intention on where they wanted to go, their torso, hips, legs and eventually feet would follow and they would naturally begin to make the turn. Yet where do most beginner ice skaters usually look? That's right, down at their feet. It is little wonder that that is where they usually wind up—down by their feet.

> We know what we are but not what we may be.
> —William Shakespeare

This is a powerful metaphor for personal growth. When we place our intention on that which we wish to accomplish, our entire being aligns with that intention. As is often said in metaphysics, "Energy flows where attention goes." The cornerstone of personal growth is to identify your goals and then place your intention on the fulfillment of that vision. Pay attention to where you place your attention, because what's got your attention has got *you!* If your attention is focused on what you want to create, then your life will naturally evolve in that direction. By the same token, if you are focused on what you do not want to manifest, your attention there will merely solidify its existence. The mind is an extremely powerful tool, shaping the way we feel, act and live. By harnessing it, you can focus your energy on creating the life you want. Getting clear on your intentions opens the way to personal growth.

Ask Yourself *This*

Who am I trying to please?

There's a tale I love to tell about an elderly man traveling from village to village with his young grandson and donkey. When they enter the first village, the villagers see the old man leading the donkey and chastise him saying, "You're a fool. At your age you shouldn't be walking, especially when you have a donkey that is fully capable of carrying you." Taking their statements to heart, the old man gets on the donkey with his grandson following behind and proceeds to the next village. Upon reaching this village, the villagers look at the little boy and ask the old man incredulously, "How could you be so heartless as to make your poor grandson walk? You should let him ride the donkey, as he is obviously tired." So the old man dismounts and places his grandson on the donkey's back. But at the next village, the people glare at the little boy and admonish him, "You are so disrespectful! How could you even think to make your grandfather walk at his age?" To placate the villagers, the old man and his grandson decide to both ride the donkey. As soon as they reach the following village, though, these villagers look at the tired donkey and accuse the old man and his grandson of being the cruelest people they have ever met. "How could you make that poor donkey bear the weight of both of you?" they ask. The boy and the old man get off the donkey. Alas, the old man is seen carrying the donkey to the next village.

There are certainly times when it is appropriate to put another's needs or wants before your own, but part of personal growth is understanding who you are trying to please and why. To grow into our full potential, it is often necessary to let go of our attachment to others' opinions of us. This does not mean we shouldn't care about the feelings of other people or that we should ignore constructive criticism. It simply means that it is impossible to please everyone all of the time. If we repress our own needs, it will come back to hurt us later. Even trying to please one person can be limiting if that is our primary focus. Instead, we should strive to express our most authentic selves as fully as possible.

> I don't know the key to success, but the key to failure is trying to please everyone.
> —Bill Cosby, Comedian

> To thine own self be true, and it must follow, as the night the day, thou canst not then be false to any man.
> —William Shakespeare

Things are rarely black or white. Trying to please only ourselves can be just as limiting as trying to please everyone else. If we only heed our own desires and wishes, we may miss our God-given opportunities to be loving, generous and kind to others.

Ask yourself, "Who am I trying to please?" Then realize that you please yourself and others most when you express the most loving, joyous and authentic you. Let go of living your life to please others and instead focus on being the best self you can be. In so doing, you will likely delight yourself and others—but more importantly, you'll more fully express the divine potential within you.

Ask Yourself *This*

What am I resisting?

In metaphysics we know that "what we resist persists." While we would all prefer to eliminate or push away unpleasant circumstances in our lives, viewing them as purely negative and resisting them is stressful and counterproductive. Resistance also robs us of powerful opportunities for personal growth, for everything that comes into our lives is here to teach us something. Fighting against our would-be teachers impedes our evolution. Instead, we can see negative moments as opportunities to learn and grow. Rather than fighting them, we can learn to accept and even welcome them when they arise.

A few years ago, I took up aikido. A Japanese martial art developed by Morihei Ueshiba, *aikido* is often translated as "the Way of unifying (with) life energy," or "the Way of harmonious spirit." I did not enroll for either self-defense or physical fitness reasons; I took up aikido for spiritual reasons. I wanted to physically experience some of the spiritual principles I had been practicing for decades—principles such as nonresistance, being fully present and aware in the "now" moment, and being an open conduit for the flow of (divine) energy and true power.

> Your spirit is the true shield … Cast off limiting thoughts and return to true emptiness. Stand in the midst of the Great Void. This is the secret of the Way of a Warrior.
>
> Ultimately, you must forget about technique. The further you progress, the fewer teachings there are. The Great Path is really No Path.
>
> —Morihei Ueshiba, Founder of Aikido

The martial art of aikido embodies all these principles but particularly the principle of nonresistance. In aikido, when you are met with an attack, the goal is to not resist. Fighting the attack results in a power struggle, and the stronger force will prevail. Aikido transcends that. The attack is seen as a gift, as it provides you with energy which, though initially destructive, can be tapped into and used.

Thus one is taught in aikido to acknowledge, welcome and blend with the motion of the attacker; then redirect the force of the attack rather than opposing it. This actually requires minimal physical energy on the part of the aikidoist, since he "leads" the attacker's momentum using entering and blending movements to reach a resolution that is beneficial to both the aikidoist and the attacker. This blending with negative energy results in a seamless transition from an attack that was originally perceived as negative to a resolution which is not only positive but causes both participants to grow. By contrast, resistance and pure physical force, which are aimed at conquest rather than resolution, can never produce such results.

Though few of the things we resist in our lives are aimed at harming us physically, the principles of aikido also apply to the mental and emotional challenges we face.

Who or what are you resisting? Instead of blocking it, consider viewing it as a gift to be welcomed, met and transmuted rather than opposed. Its energy can be transmuted into something beneficial. Recognize that no matter how ugly, difficult or negative a situation may be, it has something to teach you. There is something you can learn from it. There will always be occurrences that we want to push away or resist. But since we can't stop them, doesn't it make sense to find an element of good in them? We can allow our problems to become our teachers, fostering our personal growth. They are meant for just that.

Ask Yourself *This*

Who or what am I blaming?

Examining where we place blame reveals the level of our personal growth. It is easy to blame other people or circumstances—but your life does not happen *to* you; it happens *through* you. Your thoughts, actions and choices create your life experience. Realizing that you are responsible for the quality of your life is the cornerstone of personal and spiritual growth.

Mary and Bill had been married for 50 years and were celebrating their golden anniversary at a special party in their honor. Bill lifted his glass to toast Mary, saying, "Mary, I've been thinking about how you've been by my side all these years through thick and thin. When we almost lost the farm because of the drought, you were right there. Then when I took that bad fall on the ice and broke my hip, you were right there beside me again. When we lost most of our savings in that bad investment, there you were … right beside me. And you know, Mary, I've been thinking about it … you must be really bad luck!"

> Every person, all the events of your life are there because you have drawn them there. What you choose to do with them is up to you.
> —Richard Bach, Novelist

> When you blame others, you give up your power to change.
> —Dr. Robert Anthony, Educator

> It's only our story that keeps us from knowing that we always have everything we need.
> —Byron Katie, Author, Workshop Facilitator

Bill doesn't quite get it, does he? It's much more appealing to blame others than to take responsibility. While the thought of taking full responsibility for everything in your life (both positive and negative) can be sobering, accepting it is immensely empowering. Blaming someone or something for the condition of your life may free you of responsibility, but it also means you are powerless to change it. In blaming others, you give up the power to change your life. This doesn't mean we should blame ourselves instead of others. It simply means we recognize the power within us and channel it for good. Taking responsibility allows us to take charge of our lives.

For those of us who have not yet realized our ability to create our life experience, this is an epiphany. The leap from thinking life is happening to me to knowing life is happening through me and by me is a life-changing leap. Asking yourself, "Who or what am I blaming?" will help you make that leap, move you out of victimhood, and prepare you for tremendous personal growth.

Ask Yourself *This*

What does this tell me about myself?

This question epitomizes the process of personal growth. It reveals that, no matter how far we feel we have come, there is always more to learn. Growth is continuous. We always have room to grow. When we regress to a way of thinking and acting that does not reflect the highest and best in us, we need a question to correct our course.

> Life is a mirror and will reflect back to the thinker what he thinks into it.
> —Ernest Holmes,
> Founder of Religious Science

"What does this tell me about myself?" encourages us to look at any situation as an opportunity for personal growth.

This question not only helps us grow as individuals, but also helps us resolve conflicts in our lives. What can the situations in your life tell you about yourself? This is a powerful question. It may cause you to feel vulnerable to self-criticism and ridicule as you look deeply at the places you need to grow. Because of this, it is important that you ask this question nonjudgmentally, with a sincere desire to learn about yourself and grow. It is also important to ask this question at the right time, when you are able to hear the answer.

Some time ago, I was counseling a woman who was going through some very tough times. Her world seemed to be crumbling around her. In the midst of tears she asked me, "What am I supposed to learn from this? Why is this happening? What is my lesson?" Though I truly admired her willingness to ask those tough questions, at that moment she was in so much emotional distress it was unlikely she'd be able to really hear the answer, let alone retain it. It was more important for her to clear her mind and make the decisions that had to be made. The deeper personal learning was better left for a later, less emotionally raw time when she could safely explore those questions.

I stopped her and told her that this was not the time to ask those questions. In addition, asking that question when she was in such tremendous sadness would have been more harmful than helpful, as it likely would have resulted in self-doubt when she really needed strength.

When we ask, "What does this tell me about myself?" we need to be sensitive to its timeliness. If asked at the wrong time, the question will not result in the best possible answer. In addition, if we are so overwhelmed by the moment, we will be unable to truly internalize the answer we do find.

Ask Yourself This

Whom do I need to forgive?

Become thoroughly honest with yourself and hold the question, "Whom do I need to forgive?" If you hold the question sincerely, the truest answer will naturally come to you. For this reason, it is important that we don't edit, judge or argue with what comes up. Such denials are only confirmations that this is indeed what we need to work through. Don't resist it. It is a gift, an opportunity to grow.

Forgiveness is one of the most essential requisites for personal growth. There are certainly horrible things that happen in this world. There are times when we are wronged. And there are times when justice must be administered or consequences endured. But none of this negates (in fact it necessitates) the need for forgiveness. Forgiveness is not something we do for someone else; it is something we do for ourselves. Harboring resentment and hate only hurts us. If we refuse to forgive, it is we who suffer most. When we refuse to forgive, we block the flow of good in our lives.

The painting of the Last Supper is one of the great art treasures of the world. The face of Jesus—the focal point of the fresco—is spiritually as well as artistically captivating. It is said that while he was working on the face of Jesus, Leonardo da Vinci got into a nasty argument and threatened his adversary with bodily harm. Out of revenge, he painted Judas' face to look like his adversary's. When he resumed his painting, his heart was full of hatred and resentment, and try as he might, he couldn't paint Jesus' face. Realizing his anger was blocking the peace necessary for him to create, he found the man, apologized, and asked his forgiveness. Only then was he able to resume his work and paint the face of Jesus.

> In the long run, it's not a question of whether they deserve to be forgiven. You're not forgiving them for their sake. You're doing it for yourself. For your own health and well-being, forgiveness is simply the most energy-efficient option. It frees you from the incredibly toxic, debilitating drain of holding a grudge. Don't let these people live rent free in your head. If they hurt you before, why let them keep doing it year after year in your mind? It's not worth it. But it takes heart effort to stop it. You can muster that heart power to forgive them as a way of looking out of yourself. It's one thing you can be totally selfish about.
>
> —Doc Childre
> and Howard Martin,
> *The HeartMath Solution*

Withholding our forgiveness, no matter how justified we think we are, only punishes us. An unforgiving heart is a blocked heart—love can neither get in nor get out.

Where is the block in your heart? Whom do you need to forgive?

Forgiveness requires that we let go of the past, not that we condone it. It requires us to grow and not allow our internal peace to be jeopardized by hatred. You may take comfort in your justified anger, but holding on to that bitterness is unhealthy. Placing all of our energy into a negative emotion saps our happiness and peace. When we forgive, however, we are able to redirect our energy to self-healing.

Forgiveness is not easy. I have consciously practiced it for more than three decades and still have times and situations in which I have difficulty applying it. If you find you can't forgive someone or something completely, then be willing to take even a baby step. If all you can do is pray to "want to forgive," then start there. It will move you in the right direction.

> Many people are afraid to forgive because they feel they must remember the wrong or they will not learn from it. The opposite is true. Through forgiveness, the wrong is released from its emotional stranglehold on us so that we can learn from it. Through the power and intelligence of the heart, the release of forgiveness brings expanded intelligence to work with the situation more effectively.
>
> —David McArthur and Bruce McArthur, *The Intelligent Heart*

Ask Yourself This

Am I willing to let go of the size of the life I've known to have a bigger life?

I once read that when New York City was first established, it had a total of five or six streets. The city fathers knew that the easiest way to name the streets was to simply number them. They had already decided that the final street within the city limits would be called Boundary Street. In order to determine which street would eventually become Boundary Street, the city fathers speculated as to how big New York City was likely to become. They then expanded that number sufficiently to give the city plenty of room to grow. They felt sure the city would never grow beyond 19 streets so 19th Street became Boundary Street—and the city's limit. New York City now has 254 streets, 235 more than the city fathers ever thought possible.

> I firmly believe that all human beings have access to extraordinary energies and powers. Judging from accounts of mystical experience, heightened creativity, or exceptional performance by athletes and artists, we harbor a greater life than we know.
> —Jean Houston, Author

Where have you set your 19th Street? The question, "Am I willing to let go of the size of the life I've known to have a bigger life?" can catapult us to a whole new dimension of being. Unless we are willing to expand our vision for our lives, personal growth will only remain a distant dream. If, however, we have the courage to live larger, we will grow exponentially.

> It is not the mountain we conquer but ourselves.
> —Sir Edmund Hillary,
> First to Everest summit in 1953

If you were to spend 20 minutes writing about the biggest life you can imagine for yourself, what would you include? There is no cost for dreaming big, but there is a big cost for dreaming small. As you answer this question, remember that even the largest life you can imagine today does not encompass your full potential.

Don't let the size of the life you now live limit your possibilities. "When it's time to die," as Henry David Thoreau said, "let us not discover that we have never lived." Keep stretching and growing and reaching and becoming. Live your life, to the fullest, every day.

I read somewhere that as playwright George Bernard Shaw was nearing the end of his life, a reporter asked him a rather profound question. The reporter began by saying, "Mr. Shaw, you have been around some of the most famous people in the world. You are on a first-name basis with royalty, world-renowned authors, artists, teachers and dignitaries from every part of this continent." Then the reporter asked, "If you had your life to live over again and could be anybody you've ever known, who would you want to be?"

After a moment of silence Shaw replied "Sir, I would choose to be the man George Bernard Shaw could have been but never was."

Chapter Four

Ask Yourself *This*

To Build a Happier and More Meaningful Life

Why are you here? What is your purpose in this world? Author Ingrid Bengis writes in *Combat in the Erogenous Zone:*

The real questions are the ones that obtrude upon your consciousness whether you like it or not, the ones that make your mind start vibrating like a jackhammer, the ones that you "come to terms with" only to discover that they are still there. The real questions refuse to be placated. They barge into your life at the times when it seems most important for them to stay away. They are the questions asked most frequently and answered most inadequately, the ones that reveal their true natures slowly, reluctantly, most often against your will.[1]

> Very little is needed to make a happy life. It is all within yourself, in your way of thinking.
> —Marcus Aurelius, Roman Emperor

We don't seem to ponder these types of questions deeply enough, yet they are integral to our quest for meaning, purpose, and, ultimately, happiness. We all want to be happy, yet it seems to elude us. Ask yourself,

> A bird does not sing because it has an answer, it sings because it has a song.
> —Chinese Proverb

> A man is rich in proportion to the things he can afford to let alone.
> —Henry David Thoreau

"What makes me happy?" What makes you feel content, at ease, blissful? The answers that come to mind may be related to a sense of purpose or meaning. For many of us, happiness is generated by a sense of achievement, the fulfillment of a meaningful goal. We all hunger for lives that are significant. We want our lives to matter. We want to make a difference in our world. We want to do more than simply survive.

Yet we often pursue happiness in all the wrong ways. We think *things* will make us happy. But things wear out and break. Just when we figure out how to operate our new cell phone or iPod, a new version comes out. Just when we thought we'd put enough away for retirement, the stock market crashes.

No "thing," however new, shiny, beautiful or cool, can give us lasting happiness or the assurance that our life matters. Oh, a "thing" might put a smile on our faces for awhile or relieve our depression momentarily, but these feelings fade as soon the next new "thing" appears.

Lasting happiness is the by-product of living with a sense of meaning and purpose—a life lived for something bigger than oneself.

Ask Yourself *This*

What really matters to me? What do I stand for?

As a minister, I've officiated at numerous memorial services. I'm always moved when I hear how the deceased is remembered by those left behind. While the formal part of the eulogy often emphasizes the facts of the deceased's life, the informal sharing of family and friends speaks more to the deep personal impact their beloved had on their lives. They reveal what mattered most to the deceased.

To address this question for yourself, imagine attending

your own memorial service. Who do you want to be there? What do you hope they say about you? If you're a parent, what would you want your child to say about you? If you are married or in a committed relationship, what would you want your partner to say about you? How about your closest friends? Your coworkers? Your neighbors? What do you want all of these people to remember you for? As you ponder these questions, you begin to get in touch with what really matters to you and what you stand for. You can then make a personal commitment to live in a way that will make those sentiments be true.

> Be sure to put your feet in the right place, then stand firm.
> —Abraham Lincoln

> I am only one; but I am still one. I cannot do everything, but still I can do something. I will not refuse to do the something I can do.
> —Helen Keller

When you think about it, what is truly important to us is a relatively thin but very deep slice of life. Knowing the contents of that thin, deep slice allows us to live a happier, more purposeful life. When we are aware of what matters most to us, we know where to devote our time and energy. And since we are devoting ourselves to something we care deeply about, we naturally feel more fulfilled.

Once you've become clear on what matters to you and what you stand for, I encourage you to expand this question. If you have a spouse or a partner, explore this question together. As a couple, What really matters to us? As a couple, What do we stand for? As a couple, How would we like to be

> Live out of your imagination, not your history.
> —Stephen Covey, Businessman

> If we are to go forward, we must go back and rediscover those precious values—that all reality hinges on moral foundations and that all reality has spiritual control.
> —Martin Luther King Jr.

remembered? Likewise, if you have children, explore these questions with them. What really matters to us as a family? What does our family stand for? What are our core values? It is very important that children grow up knowing their family values. Values give our children a rudder with which to navigate the rivers of life. What children hear talked about and modeled at home impacts them deeply as they become adults.

Friedrich Nietzsche, the German philosopher of the late 19th century, spoke to the power of a purposeful life when he said, "He who has a 'why' to live can bear almost any 'how.'" When we know what is important to us and what we stand for, we can indeed handle any "how." The power in our purpose is stronger than any doubt. The details of how we are going to do something are important, but we get far fewer grey hairs asking ourselves "How?" than we do when we ask ourselves "Why?"

The power in asking "What really matters to me? What do I stand for?" is that it forces us to clarify what we hold dearest and see as most significant in our lives. In the words of writer/poet Rachel Snyder, we "sharpen … our viewpoint on what's truly important—and keep everything else a blur."

Ask Yourself *This*

Who paid the price for me?

This question is not intended to be asked from a place of guilt or obligation, but rather from one of appreciation. Appreciation and happiness are sister emotions. When we are grateful, we focus less on what we lack and more on what we love. When I stop and ask myself, "Who paid the price for me?" I am humbled in a most beautiful way. This humility is not a feeling of unworthiness but one of respect. I find myself thinking about, remembering and appreciating those who came before me whom I will never know personally, but to whom I owe so much. It is for this very reason that though I stand for the peaceful and nonviolent resolution of conflict, I am brought to tears when I stand on the beaches of Normandy, France, and consider the events of D-Day, or walk through Arlington Cemetery in Washington, D.C. I cry when I read the Declaration of Independence because I know that in enjoying the freedoms I do today, I stand on the shoulders of those who paid an immense price to secure those freedoms.

> At times our own light goes out and is rekindled by a spark from another person. Each of us has cause to think with deep gratitude of those who have lighted the flame within us.
> —Albert Schweitzer

Albert Einstein expressed it beautifully when he said, "A hundred times a day I remind myself that my inner and outer lives are based on the labors of other people, living and dead, and that I must exert myself in order to give in the same measure as I have received and am still receiving."

"Who paid the price for me?" Asking this question reminds us that we are the beneficiaries of so much more than we typically remember. It also inspires us to consider what we can give on behalf of those who will come after us.

In his book, *A Better Way to Live*, author Og Mandino tells an inspiring story illustrating the point that no one makes it through life entirely on their own. It is the story of Albert and Albrecht Durer, two brothers who lived in Nuremburg, Germany, in the 14th and 15th centuries. Their parents

> This is the true joy of life, the being used up for a purpose recognized by yourself as a mighty one; being a force of nature instead of a feverish, selfish little clot of ailments and grievances, complaining that the world will not devote itself to making you happy. I am of the opinion that my life belongs to the community, and as long as I live, it is my privilege to do for it what I can.
> —George Bernard Shaw

had 18 children and daily life was difficult because money was scarce and there were so many mouths to feed. But, youth being youth, dreams were not restrained by the scarcity of money or an overcrowded home. Albert and Albrecht dreamt of attending an art academy and becoming artists. Art was their passion and love, yet they both knew their parents could never afford to send them to art school. Their father was already working multiple jobs just so the family could survive.

Being resourceful and self-reliant, however, the two brothers devised a plan. They would toss a coin and the loser of the coin toss would go down and work in the coal mines for four years and from his earnings fund the other's education. At the end of the four years they would swap. The brother who had already gone to the art academy would send the proceeds from the sale of his art to put the other brother through school.

Albrecht won the coin toss and so had the opportunity to go off and study art first while his brother went to work in the coal mines. It became apparent very quickly that Albrecht had tremendous talent. He was skilled in many different media. With his talent in oil painting, wood sculpting and carving, and silver work he soon surpassed the abilities of his teachers.

After Albrecht's graduation, a great homecoming was held in the community to celebrate his success. At the end of the gathering Albrecht stood up with glass in hand to toast his brother and to acknowledge that if it were not for him, he would never have been able to pursue his dream. Now it was Albert's turn. Albert stood to return the toast with tears in his eyes and sorrowfully explained that it was too late for him. The four years he spent working in the mines had caused every finger on each hand to be crushed at least once and contributed to arthritis that was so severe he could barely hold his glass and return his brother's toast.

> If you look deeply into the palm of your hand, you will see your parents and all generations of your ancestors. All of them are alive in this moment.
> —Thich Nhat Hanh

Albrecht did not let his brother's sacrifice for him go unnoticed. While you may not recognize the name Albrecht Durer, if you have been to any of the world's major art museums, you've seen his masterpieces. One iconic work of art, most people would recognize immediately: It is a gray and white brush drawing on blue-grounded paper commonly called "Praying Hands." To honor his brother, Albrecht asked Albert to place his hands together in a prayerful position so that he could sketch the broken yet beautiful hands that made his dream possible. He simply called this work "The Hands."[2]

Living with the question "Who paid the price for me?" gently in our hearts increases the gratefulness we feel and inspires us to live a life of meaning and purpose so that we, too, leave a legacy of love behind us.

Ask Yourself *This*

What do I have to give?

This is a natural progression from "Who paid the price for me?" as we move from receiving to giving. Futurist, author and lecturer Barbara Marx Hubbard often speaks about our need to contribute who and what we are to the world. She says the challenge is that the world may not yet recognize or know how to receive our unique and special gifts.

Nevertheless, there is something within you that wants and needs to be expressed and offered to the world. Your ultimate happiness and fulfillment depend on your giving it. You have something to give that your world is desperate to receive. It doesn't matter whether your world is the family you love, the class you teach, the office in which you work, or the spiritual community in which you participate. You have something special to give that is needed! I deeply believe that each one of us in our own way has something to contribute to create

> How can I be useful, of what service can I be? There is something inside me, what can it be?
> —Vincent Van Gogh

> If something comes to life in others because of you, then you have made an approach to immortality.
> —Norman Cousins

> The sole meaning of life is to serve humanity.
> —Leo Tolstoy

a world that works for everyone. At times we may feel ill-equipped; we may not know where or how to begin. But none of that changes the fact that we are driven to express in form what we already are in essence. True happiness comes from achieving that intention.

Take some time to consider who you are and what you have to offer. Examine what makes you unique. Explore what you are eager and excited to share with others. Look at how you express your gifts, when you express them, and who you are when you give them. We do not give because of what we hope to receive; we give because of what we become when we give freely.

Not everything that is called "giving" is truly giving. We've all received gifts with strings attached. Such gifts aren't true gifts and the receipt of them often makes us feel manipulated and used. Contrast that with how it feels to be given a gift from one who has no motivation other than to share freely out of the fullness of who and what they are. Such an exchange blesses both the receiver and the giver.

One of my favorite books is a biography about Walter Russell titled *The Man Who Tapped the Secrets of the Universe,* by Glenn Clark. Walter Russell was a man of many and varied talents. He enjoyed success in painting, sculpture, music and philosophy, in addition to authoring two books, *The Secret of Light* and *The Message of the Divine Iliad*, which laid out his unified theory of physics.

As a young man, Walter took a job as a bellboy in a prestigious hotel for the meager salary of eight dollars a month though he was told he might expect to receive as much as $100 in tips for the summer season. However, when the first guest offered him a tip, something deep within told him not to take it. Later that day, when he reflected upon what had happened and probed the inner voice more deeply, he had a vision. "I'll be the only bellboy in existence who never took a tip! And I'll be the best bellboy the world ever knew. I'll pledge myself to give the most joyful and cheerful service that ever a bellboy gave!"

From that moment he was the epitome of top-notch customer service, going above and beyond at every opportunity and responding cheerfully to every special request. When asked why he refused to accept tips, he explained that he loved his work and he was already paid for it. Guests were amazed by his service and expressed their delight by inviting him to join them at their special dinner parties and yachting trips. When the management explained that such interactions between guests and servants were not allowed, the guests argued that if an exception was not made for Walter, they would never return to the hotel again. Guests took a particular interest in the sketching and painting that Walter did

> If you knew what I know about the power of giving, you would not let a single meal pass without sharing it in some way.
> —Buddha, *Dhammapada*
>
> When you cease to make a contribution, you begin to die.
> —Eleanor Roosevelt

during his spare time and by the end of the summer rather than earning $100 in tips he received checks amounting to $850 for his pictures—and five offers of legal adoption![3]

What do you have to give? What talents, abilities, attributes and ways of being can you offer to others? When you give of yourself deeply and without thought of repayment, you experience giving's own reward: the boundless joy and satisfaction that come from freely expressing oneself.

Ask Yourself *This*

What if this could be easy and fun?

What creates more joy, more happiness, more contentment than a simple sense of fun? For many years I enjoyed a deep and rich prayer partnership with another Unity minister, Rev. Richard Rogers. Frequently, when I would share about some difficulty I was going through or about feeling overwhelmed by my work at the church and responsibilities at home, Richard would stop me and ask: "What if you just let this be easy and fun? What if you just stop for a moment and allow this to be a little bit easier, a little bit more fun?" While I wasn't always successful in doing it, I always appreciated the question because it helped me shift my perspective.

> The really efficient laborer will be found not to crowd his day with work, but will saunter to his task surrounded by a wide halo of ease and leisure.
> —Henry David Thoreau

We all have routine tasks to do that we don't particularly like. Perhaps it's doing the laundry, washing dishes, shopping for groceries, paying bills or mowing the lawn. If the tasks are ours to do anyway, why not find a way to make them more enjoyable? This question sparks our creativity and adds joy to out lives.

I love this additional story of Walter Russell, who, when faced with having to mow his very large lawn at his splendid country home, decided to make the task more fun. Instead of mowing the lawn in typical straight rows, he made a game of it. He would mow patterns and designs in the grass as he cut it and then gradually eliminate the patterns until all the grass had been cut. He took a routine task he wasn't particularly fond of and made it easy and fun![4]

May Rowland, former director of Silent Unity (Unity's 24/7 prayer ministry), devoted an entire chapter in her book

Dare to Believe! to a similar practice. She suggested that when we feel overwhelmed, burdened or worried, we should give the situation "the light touch ... the touch of light." She wrote, "Our success lies not so much in how we handle the situation, but in how we handle ourselves. We are able to handle each situation that arises easily, smoothly, and harmoniously—with the light touch—when we learn to control and direct our thinking about each situation. Our strength emerges from our way of thought."[5]

> Laugh at yourself and at life. Not in the spirit of derision or whining self-pity, but as a remedy, a miracle drug, that will ease your pain, cure your depression, and help you to put in perspective that seemingly terrible defeat and worry with laughter at your predicaments, thus freeing your mind to think clearly toward the solution that is certain to come.
> —Og Mandino, Author

We will always have to deal with situations in life that are less than pleasant. No matter how long we have been on a spiritual path, no matter what church, synagogue, mosque or background we've come from, life happens. There are always circumstances we hadn't planned or asked for (at least not consciously) and that we'd rather not have to deal with. Living consciously doesn't change that. But it does fundamentally shift how we respond to such things. Asking yourself, "What if this could be easy and fun?" is a powerful way to connect with a deeper place of peace and centeredness in your day-to-day living.

Ask Yourself This

Is it "Good morning, God!" or "Good God! Morning!"?

This question epitomizes the search for happiness. While the world around us may have an impact on our feelings, the ultimate determinant of our happiness is our attitude. Regardless of what is happening outside us, our perception and outlook determine how we respond to it. This is a fundamental yet powerful practice.

I heard my first Unity minister, Rev. Robert Stevens, tell this story: A seasoned truck driver took on a young man as his apprentice. The senior truck driver wanted his trainee to become acquainted with the work of truck driving so he took the junior truck driver out for a 12-hour drive. When the trip was finally over, they stopped for dinner. While waiting for their meal, the apprentice looked at the older man in disbelief and said, "I don't understand how you still look as refreshed and alive as you did this morning, while I am absolutely wiped out. What's the difference?"

> Your living is determined not so much by what life brings to you as by the attitude you bring to life; not so much by what happens to you as by the way your mind looks at what happened.
> —Khalil Gibran

The old man just looked at him and said, "The difference is simply this: While you went to work this morning, I went for a drive in the country." They drove the same truck, traveled the same number of miles, faced the same traffic challenges, but each had a completely different way of experiencing it.

Happiness and purpose make life a little easier and a little brighter. While we often can't change life's circumstances, we absolutely can change our reactions to and perceptions of them. How do you live your life? When you wake up, do you shout "Good morning, God!" or do you grumble "Good God! Morning!"?

Chapter Five

Ask Yourself *This*

To Improve Your Relationships

The Sufis tell the story of a man who in his youth wanted to change the world. He was passionate, and he prayed every day to be successful. But he made no progress. As the years went by and he approached middle age, he changed his prayer. Rather than praying to change the world, he decided to narrow his circle. His daily prayer became, "God, I haven't been successful at changing the world. So please help me at least be able to change the people I live with, the people I see each and every day." Still he failed. As he approached old age, he changed his prayer one last time. This time his prayer became, "God, I haven't been successful in changing the world and I haven't even been successful at changing the people I live with. Let me change myself." And, of course, with that as his prayer, he was successful.

> You must not lose faith in humanity. Humanity is an ocean; if a few drops of the ocean are dirty, the ocean does not become dirty.
> —Mohandas Gandhi

> If you were going to die soon and had only one phone call you could make, who would you call and what would you say? And why are your waiting?
> —Stephen Levine, Author

Even with years of practice on the spiritual path, it can still be hard not to make others our project—especially the "others" with whom we live and work. Sometimes our intentions are sincere, and we are truly wanting to help. But often, if we're honest with ourselves, we're motivated more by the thought that if only they would change, we could finally be happy.

Trying to change others to be the way we think they should be or the way we want them to be is a recipe for disaster. No one likes to be another person's project. And while it is certainly true that we can and do influence each other, lasting change only happens when an individual makes that choice for him or herself. The seven questions in this chapter will go a long way toward helping you improve your relationships, by starting with yourself.

Ask Yourself *This*

Who am I trying to change?

Who is your project? Your irascible neighbor? Your critical co-worker? Who are you trying to make over? Your noncommunicative spouse? Your judgmental mother-in-law? Who are you wishing and praying and visualizing would be different? Be honest, now. I bet there's someone!

Refuse to buy into the temptation to rationalize your answer by saying things like: "But I just want them to change because I love them so much" (you probably do love them, that's not the issue) or "I just know that if they meditated and prayed, they'd be better off" (they probably would; meditation and prayer have been proven to be

> Some of the biggest challenges in relationships come from the fact that most people enter a relationship in order to get something: they're trying to find someone who's going to make them feel good. In reality, the only way a relationship will last is if you see your relationship as a place that you go to give, and not a place that you go to take.
> —Anthony Robbins, Author

> Each relationship nurtures a strength or weakness within you.
> —Mike Murdock, Author

effective) or "I just know if they followed a low-fat diet, dropped that extra weight and lowered their cholesterol, they'd be happier" (this may be true too). Refuse the temptation to justify your answer and just stay with the question. Regardless of the reasons, who are you trying to change?

Though you've undoubtedly heard it before, it bears repeating: People don't change because we want them to; they change because *they* want to. It doesn't matter how clever, how noble, how skilled, how manipulative we might be, people only make lasting changes when they are willing and ready to do so. Period.

A wise man once said: "A man convinced against his will is a man of the former opinion still!" We can manipulate, we can love, we can pray someone into a temporary change, but I promise you it will be temporary. As soon as we remove ourselves from the picture, reduce the pressure or shift our focus, they will go right back to where they were before—and probably breathe a sigh of relief that we've finally backed off! Lasting personal change happens only when the pain of staying the same is greater than the pain of changing.

We can certainly help and support others to change, but only when the time is right. Have you noticed that when you jump in uninvited (no matter what the motivation), your efforts are seldom met warmly? But when another reaches out to you and invites you in, saying, "I'm struggling, and I could use some help," or "I'd like your opinion," or "I'd like your help in making a change," the exchange is entirely different. Then, whatever you have learned along your life's journey can be shared, and it will likely be helpful and appreciated.

I read a very tender and moving story in *Guideposts* magazine that beautifully illustrates acceptance. A family consisting of the grandmother, mother, father and children were having dinner together. The grandmother was always a bit eccentric and this mealtime was no exception. She started to eat her peas in a most unusual way. She took her knife, stuck it into the pile of peas and despite her shaking hand, successfully brought the knife to her mouth and ate all the peas with the exception of one which rolled off. The grandkids were all giggling and broke into applause at her accomplishment. "Wow, Grandma, that was really, really good, but that was really weird. Why are you eating your peas like that?" they asked.

Grandma explained that when she was a little girl growing up on a farm during the Great Depression, her family would often feed hungry strangers at their dinner table. One time a hungry hobo who had hopped a train found their little farm and knocked on the door. Grandmother's father invited the man to join the family for dinner. After grace was said the family waited, as was their custom, for the guest to start eating first. Their guest was very, very hungry. On the table was a plate piled high with peas. The guest put a large serving on his plate and thrust his knife into the pile of peas. Hand quivering, he managed to get the peas to his mouth and finished his entire plate of peas that way. Grandma was a little girl at the time, and she and her sister started giggling at his strange behavior. They had never seen anyone eat peas that way. Then Father gave them that parental "look" and they stopped giggling instantly. Father then took his knife and began eating his peas the same way his guest had. After their guest left, Father reprimanded them for their rude behavior. He explained that this man had been a guest in their home and did not know their customs or manners. It was up to them to help him feel welcomed and protect his dignity, not to embarrass him.

What a touching example of acceptance—of not trying to change another or of assuming your way is the better way. In big and small ways, we try to make other people be like us instead of learning to accept—and enjoy—the great and wonderful diversity of human expression. Leo Stein, art collector and brother of Gertrude Stein, says, "The wise man questions the wisdom of others because he questions his own; the foolish man, because it is different from his own."

Ask Yourself *This*

How much room do I give people to grow and change?

Do you hold people hostage to their past? Do you hold people hostage to their last mistake or their worst fault? If you've ever been held hostage in such a way, you know it doesn't feel very good. Are you as bad as the worst mistake you've ever made? Of course you aren't. Are you as bad as your worst shortcoming or inadequacy? No, you're not. There's much more to you than the worst mistake you've ever made or the prickliest part of your personality.

Some time ago I saw a poster that captured this idea well. It portrayed a little boy of about six or seven. His hair was disheveled, his T-shirt was soiled, his jeans ripped (not as a fashion statement like they are today) and his shoelaces were untied. He was standing with a baseball bat in his hand looking at the broken window his baseball had just flown through. The caption read: "Please be patient with me. God isn't finished with me yet."

There's a little bit of that boy in all of us. We can all say about ourselves: "Please be patient with me. God isn't finished with me yet." This question is aimed at fostering that same kind of patience, tolerance and kindheartedness toward everyone else.

> Piglet sidled up to Pooh from behind. "Pooh!" he whispered. "Yes, Piglet?" "Nothing," said Piglet, taking Pooh's paw. "I just wanted to be sure of you."
> —A.A. Milne, Author

We in Unity (and in all of New Thought, for that matter) believe that humankind—all of it—is inherently good, not inherently flawed. We believe that the spark of the divine, the God Presence, indwells each and every one of us. We didn't put it there (God did), and we can't get rid of it (thank God!). However, we can hide it, ignore it, cover it up or dumb it down. Nevertheless, it is still there, waiting to be expressed. You are not born in original sin (which is a church teaching, not a Biblical one). You are born in original blessing—in the image and the likeness of God. We all are.

This Truth isn't a permission slip to stay stuck at our current level of expression, but rather an invitation to give ourselves—and others—plenty of room to grow and change. And when growth and change do occur, it is time to celebrate! Even the baby steps! That's what helps us keep going.

Do you hold people hostage to their past? Do you have a good memory for what they didn't do, the mistakes they made or where they fell short—but a poor memory for the good they've done? My minister friend Robert Stevens says we could take a lesson from a story he read about John D. Rockefeller.

> If you treat an individual ... as if he were what he ought to be and could be, he will become what he ought to be and could be.
> —Johann Wolfgang von Goethe, Poet

When John D. Rockefeller was CEO of Standard Oil, one of his executives made a colossal mistake costing the company more than $2 million. That day no one wanted to have anything to do with Rockefeller because they all knew his temper. Everyone kept their distance from him except one executive who absolutely had to meet with Rockefeller that day. Though he wasn't the one who had made the costly error, he was nonetheless prepared to be the target of considerable misplaced anger. When he entered Rockefeller's office he saw him at his desk scribbling furiously on a piece of paper. Rockefeller looked up and said, "I suppose you've heard the bad news."

The executive said, "Yes. I know we've just lost $2 million. I guess you're going to fire him."

"Fire him?" Rockefeller questioned. "Definitely not. We've just invested $2 million in his education. And I've been sitting here all morning reminding myself of his good qualities and the times he's done well and saved the company money."

What a powerful lesson for all of us. When we're angry and upset—even when it appears justified—our field of vision can narrow so much that we only see the failings, faults and mistakes in the other and not the fullness of who they are. Giving people room to change and grow requires the mature understanding that we are all going to make mistakes from time to time but that we are more than the mistakes we make.

Ask Yourself *This*

How safe is it for people to walk through the corridors of your mind?

I love this question because it challenges us to go deeper. Many of us have worked hard to improve our communication skills. We've taken classes and workshops or read books ranging from how to talk so others will listen, to how to listen so others will talk to us. But this question challenges us to go even deeper. It challenges us to examine the silent, private thoughts we *think* about others. How safe is it for people to "walk through the corridors of your mind?" If the thoughts you think about others were broadcast over a public address system, would you feel the need to run and hide, or would you feel peaceful and happy?

As students of consciousness, we know that thought is formative. Consciousness creates. So even though we may not verbalize the negative judgments, silent prejudices belittling thoughts we hold in our minds, they do in fact have an impact (clearly on us in the emotional toxicity they introduce into our bodies, and certainly on others in the energetic vibration such thoughts give off). These thoughts generate feelings and emotions, and these feelings and emotions extend beyond us in a measurable way. Research at the Institute of HeartMath has shown that an electromagnetic field produced through the heart can be detected as much as five feet from the individual.

> What you see and hear depends a good deal on where you are standing; it also depends on what sort of person you are.
> —C.S. Lewis, Author

It's probably pretty safe for people who are similar to you to walk through the corridors of your mind. But how safe is it for those who are very different from you to take that walk? What is the quality of the silent conversation you hold in your mind about them?

> We don't see things as they are, we see things as we are.
> —Anais Nin, Author

> If you judge people, you have no time to love them.
> —Mother Teresa

I do a fair amount of traveling, so I am in airports quite a lot. Airports are great places to people watch and are often filled with the most colorful people imaginable— literally and figuratively. I've seen people with hair dyed every color of the rainbow and styled in the most unique ways. I've seen others with tattoos covering every visible inch of their bodies (and I suspect they're covering much of what's not visible!). I'm amazed at the places and styles of body piercings and always wonder how much the piercing hurt.

Such situations provide a rich opportunity to learn if we are paying attention. Not outer attention, but inner attention. The spiritual richness of the experience is not in what we are seeing in the "other" but what our judging reveals about us and how safe the "other" is in the corridors of our mind. If they are safe in our mind, then even though we may have a personal definition of beauty that differs from theirs, we can take in what we see without judgment and without making up a story about them or evaluating their character or intelligence based on their appearance. Whether our judgments are about sexual orientation, race, body piercings, hair color, style or fashion, they always reveal more about ourselves than those we are judging. Admitting that takes spiritual maturity. Overcoming it takes spiritual discipline.

Ask Yourself This

Do I have the full picture?

An old fable tells of a Persian king who wanted to discourage his four sons from criticizing others. So he sent his oldest son on a journey in winter to see a mango tree. When spring came, he sent the next oldest son on the same journey to see the mango tree. In the summer, the third son was sent, and the youngest went to see the tree in the fall.

He then called them all together to describe the mango tree. The first son said it was like an old burnt stump. The second described it as beautiful with lacy green leaves. The third said its blossoms were as beautiful as the rose. The youngest said its fruit was like a pear. "Each of you is right," the king said, "for each of you saw it in a different season. Remember this lesson: Judge not, for you may not have the full picture or know the whole truth."

> The eye sees only what the mind is prepared to comprehend.
> —Henri Bergson, Philosopher

> Better keep yourself clean and bright; you are the window through which you must see the world.
> —George Bernard Shaw

How different our relationships would be and how different our lives would be if we challenged ourselves more often with this question. It would certainly keep us from jumping so often to premature and faulty conclusions. It would definitely soften our interactions with one another and go a long way in helping us be more loving and less judgmental.

"Do I have the full picture?" is not just about making sure we remember there are always two sides to every story or, in the absence of information, refraining from jumping to conclusions. It is also about learning to look further, wider and deeper while we expand our awareness and enlarge the picture frame around our "personal world," so to speak.

On Friday, January 12, 2009, in the middle of the morning rush hour in the Washington metro at L'Enfant Plaza, the *Washington Post* conducted a most interesting experiment "in context, perception and priorities … In a banal setting at an inconvenient time, would beauty transcend?"[1]

For just under an hour a man sat leaning against the wall and played six classical masterpieces; 1097 people passed by, most of them on their way to work. Three minutes went by before anything happened, and then a middle-aged male passerby slowed his pace a bit and looked to see where the music was coming from, then continued to walk on. Another minute passed before the violinist received his first donation. A dollar bill was thrown into the open violin case by a woman who continued to walk on by. It wasn't until six minutes into the performance that anyone actually stopped for a few minutes to really listen to the exquisite music being played.

In the end, when all was tallied, only seven people stopped what they were doing to listen for a minute or more and just $32.17 was given by 27 people (which included $20 given by the only person who actually recognized the violinist).

The violinist was Joshua Bell, considered to be one of the best violinists in the world. He began his 45-minute performance with Johann Sebastian Bach's "Chaconne," which is considered one of the most difficult violin pieces to master, on a 1710 Stradivarius worth over $3.5 million. Just days before playing incognito in the metro he sold out at a theater in Boston where merely pretty good seats went for $100 each.[2]

In busyness and hurry, we can miss a lot that is important, valuable, precious and beautiful. In your relationships, in your interactions with others, challenge yourself often with the question "Do I have the full picture?" It will heighten your awareness and broaden your vision.

Ask Yourself *This*

How do I show up when I get a "no"?

It is emotionally and psychologically healthy to ask for what you want. In James 4:2 (KJV) we are told "Ye have not because ye ask not." In his book *Prescriptions for Happiness*, Ken Keyes Jr. says that to "ask for what you want, but don't demand it"[3] is one of the prescriptions for happiness. Asking is important, but not all our requests will be filled. How we handle ourselves when we get a "no" instead of a "yes" says a lot about our spiritual and emotional maturity. It gives us a snapshot of our emotional intelligence.

> Whilst thou livest, keep a good tongue in thy head.
> —William Shakespeare

> Be nice to people on your way up because you might meet'em on your way down.
> —Jimmy Durante, Comedian

At The Unity Center in San Diego, we look at this very closely when we evaluate candidates for leadership positions. It is important to us to not only know that potential leaders can handle the responsibilities of the position, but also that they can handle themselves when things are not going their way or to their liking. We want to know how they show up when they get a "no."

In a recent public workshop, Howard Martin, executive vice president of the Institute of HeartMath, made the bold statement: "Regulating emotions is the next frontier in human evolution." I agree. And I would add that how we show up when we are given a "no" reveals some of the edges of our personal frontier.

How do you show up with your spouse if he or she doesn't want to see the movie you want to see? How do you show up if your boss denies your vacation request? How do you show up if a sales clerk tells you she can't refund your money without a receipt? How do you show up in your spiritual community if your idea for a new program is rejected? How do you show up when you don't like the answer?

How you handle yourself when you get a "no" reveals a lot about how much you've grown and how much you've yet to grow.

I'm not much of a sports fan, but I am a fan of anyone who conducts themselves with dignity and class in difficult situations. Babe Ruth was certainly a baseball legend, hitting 714 home runs in the course of his career. One of the many amazing stories told about him is that toward the end of his career, there was one particular game where the Babe was not playing well at all. Largely because of errors he made while out in the field, the other team scored five runs. He was told to leave the field, and as he was heading toward the dugout, the Great Babe was booed. In the middle of all the booing, a young boy jumped the fence, ran onto the field and to the dugout. He grabbed Babe Ruth around the leg and hugged him, saying "I still love you." Babe Ruth patted him on the head and gave him a big hug. The entire stadium fell quiet. The crowd saw two heroes: a little boy who didn't hold the Babe to a really bad game and a baseball player who, despite a very public and humiliating "no," still showed up with class.

Ask Yourself *This*

What yardstick am I using?

Here's a tall tale to consider: Two Irish laborers were doing road work outside a house of prostitution. Soon the local Protestant minister came along, pulled down his hat, and walked into the building. In shock, Patrick said to Danny, "Did you see who just went in there? Ah, but what can you expect? He's a Protestant, isn't he?"

A short while later, a rabbi arrived on the scene. He took off his yarmulke, pulled his collar up and walked in too. Patrick turned to Danny again. "What a shocking example for a religious leader to give his people!"

Finally, who should pass by but a Catholic priest. He drew his cloak around his head and slipped quickly into the building. Patrick turned to Danny once again and said, "Oh, Danny, 'tis a terrible thing, isn't it, to think that one of the girls must have taken ill?"

> Only in quiet waters do things mirror themselves undistorted. Only in a quiet mind is adequate perception of the world.
> —Hans Margolius

Same situation, very different interpretations. When we like someone, we tend to see everything they do in a favorable light. When we dislike someone, we tend to see those same actions in a less favorable light. Simply put, we're not using the same yardstick.

Consider these examples from a piece called "You or Me?" (Author unknown).

"When the other person acts that way, he's ugly … when you do it, it's just nervousness.

When she's set in her ways, she's obstinate … when you are, it's firmness.

When he doesn't like your friends, he's prejudiced … when you don't like his friends, you're showing good judgment.

When she tries to be accommodating, she's apple-polishing … but when you do it, you're using tact.

When he takes time to do things, he's dead slow … but when you take ages you are deliberate.

When she picks flaws, she's cranky … when you do it, you're discriminating."[4]

We all make mistakes. We all occasionally do stupid things or act in unskillful ways. But, as Monsignor Jim Lisante in the *Western Catholic Reporter* reminds us, "None of us wants to be judged on the occasional foolish things we do, but on our overall conduct and character."[5] So let's give each other the benefit of the doubt a little more often. Let's drop our judgment and become aware of the innate truth that we are all perfectly imperfect, doing the best we can with what we have, where we are.

Chapter Six

Ask Yourself *This*

To Release Your Inner Genius

The important thing is not to stop questioning. Curiosity has its own reason for existing. One cannot help but be in awe when he contemplates the mysteries of eternity, of life, of the marvelous structure of reality. It is enough if one tries merely to comprehend a little of this mystery every day. Never lose a holy curiosity.

—Albert Einstein

We have the power to change our world. Even the most difficult challenges on both a personal and a global scale can be solved through the collective ingenuity of human consciousness. But how do we access that ingenuity? How do we tap into our inner genius?

Think of the mind as a muscle. Like every other muscle, if we do not exercise it, it loses its strength. Just as our culture values the health and fitness of our bodies, we should hold as valuable and necessary the continual exercising and expanding of our minds. Knowledge is important, but the simple acquisition of information does little to expand

> We all have the extraordinary coded within us, waiting to be released.
> —Jean Houston, Author

> Neither lofty degree of intelligence nor imagination nor both together go to the making of genius. Love, love, love, that is the soul of genius.
> —Wolfgang Amadeus Mozart

our minds. The mind can become cluttered with useless trivia or grow rigid from little real use. On the other hand, questions expand the mind's reach and allow for new, ingenious possibilities. Consider the questions in this chapter as exercises for your mind. As you contemplate the questions on the next few pages, allow your mind to expand as you wonder "why?" The greatest discoveries in history were the result of people asking that very question.

Ask Yourself *This*

Is there another way to approach this?

The question "Is there another way to approach this?" is the crux of creative thinking. Being able to look at an old problem and see it in a fresh way is a hallmark of brilliant people. Today's problems cannot be solved with yesterday's techniques. A new approach must be taken. Consider these examples:

> The dogmas of the quiet past are inadequate to the stormy present. The occasion is piled high with difficulty, and we must rise with the occasion. As our case is new, so we must think anew and act anew.
>
> —Abraham Lincoln

Legend has it that when St. Petersburg was being laid out, the city fathers used creative thinking to remove an obstacle to their planning. During the ice age, glaciers had transferred huge boulders onto the plot of land on which the city was to be built. Consequently, when the city fathers laid out the city's beautiful boulevards, they discovered there was an enormous boulder right in the middle of one of the planned streets. Clearly, either the street needed to be rerouted, which presented an entirely new set of problems, or the boulder had to be removed. They invited anyone in the community who thought they could solve the problem to submit a bid. Since this occurred before the era of explosives and heavy machinery, all the bids involved huge numbers of men and were very expensive. All except one.

A simple peasant presented a proposal and because it was by far the least expensive, he was awarded the job. The next day, he and a very small work party showed up at the site of the boulder with nothing more than shovels, logs and rope. Curious onlookers must have wondered how so few men with such simple tools could move such a large boulder. Using the timbers, they secured the huge boulder and started digging an enormous hole next to it. When the hole was large enough, the peasants removed the supporting timbers that had kept the boulder in place and allowed it to roll into the hole. The peasants then filled the remaining space with dirt and carted the unused dirt away, and the city fathers laid the road right over the buried boulder!

Here's another example of creative problem-solving: In Germany in the 1800s, a class of primary school boys were reprimanded by their schoolmaster for being noisy and boisterous. Their punishment was to find the sum of all the numbers from one to 100. Thinking that the problem would occupy his students for a long time, the schoolmaster relaxed at his desk and observed

> Obstacles are like wild animals. They are cowards but they will bluff you if they can. If they see you are afraid of them, they are liable to spring upon you; but if you look them squarely in the eye, they will slink out of sight.
> —Orison Swett Marden, Author

> When in doubt, observe and ask questions. When certain, observe at length and ask many more questions.
> —George S. Patton

> Discovery consists of seeing what everybody has seen and thinking what nobody has thought.
> —Albert Szent-Gyorgyi, *Living Good: The Scientist Speculates*

how busily every boy was working. All except one. One boy just sat at his desk and stared intently into space. After a few minutes passed, the young student finally scribbled something on his paper, and then turned in his answer. The boy's answer—5050 —was the only one that was correct. When quizzed as to how he achieved the right answer so quickly, the boy replied, "I thought there might be some short cut, and I found one: 100 plus 1 is 101; 99 plus 2 is 101; 98 plus 3 is 101, and, if I continued the series all the way to 51 plus 50, I have 101 fifty times, which is 5050." The little boy was Carl Friedrich Gauss, who later became one of the greatest mathematicians of his time.[1]

The question, "Is there another way to approach this?" challenges us to think outside the box—to think in creative, novel and unconventional ways. As a youngster I was blessed to have a father who loved to challenge my thinking and would often give me problems that would require me to think differently. When I was still in elementary school, my dad gave me this math problem.

In a rectangular room that is 30 feet long, 12 feet high and 12 feet wide, there is a little boy spider in the middle of one 12 foot by 12 foot wall one foot below the ceiling. A little girl spider is in the middle of the opposite wall one foot above the floor. If the little girl spider remains stationary, what is the shortest distance the little boy spider must crawl to give the little girl spider a kiss?

Taking a straight route down the wall, across the floor and up, one is likely to arrive at the answer 42 feet. The little boy spider walks straight down his wall 11 feet, walks across the floor 30 feet and up the opposite wall one foot to where the little girl spider is waiting. In this case, he would have walked on just three of the six surfaces of the room. But that answer is wrong. The correct answer is 40 feet and he will have actually walked on five of the six surfaces of the room!

As far as the math is concerned, nothing more than Pythagorean's theorem for finding the hypotenuse of a right

triangle (A squared plus B squared equals C squared) is needed to solve the problem. The real challenge for most of us is not the math, but the ability to approach the problem in a different way—to get outside of our usual ways of thinking and seeing. In this case, to open up the box and flatten it out. This is what it looks like when you do:

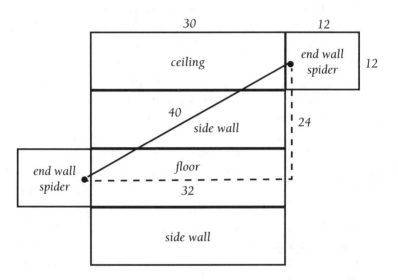

Is there another way of looking at the problems in your own life? Genius is not the product of stubbornly continuing to do things as we have always done them. Thomas Edison did *not* create the light bulb because he repeatedly tried the same solution. He was successful because he wasn't afraid to start over and try something new.

We cannot continue to attempt to solve today's problems with yesterday's methods. Our economic crisis cannot simply be healed

Humanity is acquiring all the right technology for all the wrong reasons.
—R. Buckminster Fuller

There are a thousand hacking at the branches of the evil to one who is striking at the root.
—Henry David Thoreau

through stimulus packages and taxes; there must be a change in our core values as a society and less emphasis on material wealth. The global conflicts that have erupted cannot be quieted with military force, as war has proven to only provide a temporary solution. The challenges we face are too significant and too dynamic for us to cling to the solutions of the past. As Albert Einstein said, "No problem can be solved from the same level of consciousness that created it." That's as true of the problems we face collectively as the problems we face individually. If a lasting change is to occur, we must explore a radical new way of looking at our problems and the resources available to solve them. We must release our inner genius.

The same principles can be applied to our personal problems. Our life today is the result of our past choices. If we continue to make these same choices, our trajectory will remain unchanged. The same problems we struggled through last year will reappear this year. But if we make different choices, our lives will begin to take a new direction. Just as a road that has diverged from its original course by a fraction of a degree will eventually arrive at a place hundreds of miles from its original path, so, too, will even the slightest change in our lives take us to a different place years from now. Looking at life with new eyes helps us begin making those changes.

Ask Yourself *This*
What assumptions am I making?

We all make assumptions. Many of them, and often. Undoubtedly that is why best-selling author Don Miguel Ruiz lists "Don't make assumptions" as agreement number three in his book *The Four Agreements*.[2]

Perhaps you can see yourself in this story: Two newlyweds are preparing a pot roast for their dinner. During the preparation, the wife takes the pot roast and cuts about half an inch off each end. Puzzled, her husband asks why she is cutting up the pot roast. "Well this is the way you make pot roast," she explains.

Her husband looks confused and replies, "No. I don't understand. We didn't do it that way at home."

"It's the right way to do it!" she snaps, somewhat frustrated. "My mother taught me so let's ask her."

When they call her mother and ask the proper way to make a pot roast, she says, "Well, yeah. You always cut a half inch off each end of the pot roast. Your grandmother taught me how to do that." By now the husband is getting really agitated because they never did that in his home. In exasperation he proposes that they call his wife's grandmother. When they call and tell her the subject of their dispute, the wife's grandmother begins laughing uncontrollably.

Between her peals of laughter, she blurts out, "Well honey, I only cut the ends off the pot roast because I never had a big enough pan!"

Writes Ruiz: "We have the tendency to make assumptions about everything. The problem with making assumptions is that we *believe* they are the truth. We could swear they are real. We make assumptions about what others are doing or thinking—we take it personally—then we blame them and react by sending emotional poison with our word. That is why whenever we make assumptions,

> The most erroneous stories are those we think we know best—and therefore never scrutinize or question.
> —Stephen Jay Gould, Scientist

> Our job is not to set things right, but to see things rightly.
> —Eric Butterworth, Unity Minister

> Begin challenging your own assumptions. Your assumptions are your windows on the world. Scrub them off every once in awhile, or the light won't come in.
> —Alan Alda

we're asking for problems. We make an assumption, we misunderstand, we take it personally, and we end up creating a whole big drama for nothing," he writes. "The way to keep yourself from making assumptions is to ask questions."[3]

> The greatest obstacle to discovering the shape of the earth, the continents, and the oceans was not ignorance but the illusion of knowledge.
> —Daniel J. Boorstin, Historian

I remember an incident when my son was about five or six years old. He contracted a very severe sore throat and started running a fever. After treating it for several days with vitamins and homeopathics and still seeing no signs of improvement, I decided I needed to take him to the doctor. So that night while tucking him into bed, I told him I'd made an appointment and we'd be going to the doctor in the morning. He looked petrified and immediately asked if he was going to need a shot. Since he'd had the symptoms for a few days, I honestly didn't know, and I told him I couldn't promise that the doctor wouldn't give him a shot. He pressed more and started to cry saying he didn't want a shot, it was much too scary. Trying to reassure him while still being honest, I said, "Honey, you've had shots before. Remember the ones you got right before you went to preschool?" In an instant his whole expression changed.

"Oh! You mean they'll give me the shot in my *arm*? They won't give me the shot in my throat?"

Because the pain was in his throat, Johnathon assumed that was where he'd get the shot. (I'd have been afraid of that too!)

Our assumptions are often wrong. And when unchecked, our assumptions can cause us a lot of unnecessary misery.

What assumptions are you making about your life? Your job? Other people? When we assume, we restrict our creativity and ingenuity because we are so certain of something that we do not allow ourselves to see it in a new way. A closed mind is a mind that cannot expand. Our understanding of the world was made possible by others who came before us and challenged the assumptions of their day. They include the Polish astronomer and mathematician Nicolaus Copernicus, who believed Earth revolved around a stationary sun; Jesus the Christ, who challenged the religious beliefs of his day that fostered a sense of separation between man and God; and Unity's founders, Charles and Myrtle Fillmore, who challenged the assumption that sickness was inherited.

We must be willing to be honest and do the hard inner work of examining our assumptions. Only then can we set ourselves free from their limiting grip and unlock the door to inner genius.

Ask Yourself *This*

Could they be wrong?

As a youth, I would often get frustrated when I would come home from school and ask my father for help with my homework. If I would try to explain something by saying, "Well, they say ..." my father would immediately stop me and ask "Who is they?" Or, if I told him, "It's written in the book!" he would frequently challenge me and ask, "Could it be wrong?" Though I didn't realize it at the time, my dad was modeling skills I would come to value greatly as an adult: the ability to think critically, the courage to think for myself, and the willingness to challenge the limiting beliefs of those around me. No great thinkers became successful by accepting knowledge without question. They became successful because they questioned knowledge without exception.

> The authority of those who teach is often an obstacle to those who want to learn.
> —Marcus Tullius, Roman Philosopher

"Could they be wrong?" Absolutely. Consider these amusing and amazing examples.

"Louis Pasteur's theory of germs is ridiculous fiction!"

—Pierre Pachet, Professor of physiology in Toulouse in 1873

"The wireless music box has no imaginable commercial value. Who would pay for a message sent to nobody in particular?"

—David Sarnoff's associates in response to his urgings for investment in radio in the 1920s

"But what is it good for?"

—An engineer at IBM in 1968 commenting on the microchip

"We told Atari, 'We've got this amazing thing built with some of your parts. What do you think about funding us? Or we'll give it to you. We just want to do it. Pay our salary; we'll come to work for you.' They said 'No.'"

—Apple Computer founder Steve Jobs on attempts to get Atari interested in his and Steve Wozniak's personal computer

And my personal favorite, from Charles H. Duell, commissioner of the U.S. Office of Patents, in 1899: *"Everything that can be invented has been invented."*

I have developed a personal practice that I have found to be very beneficial. I call it "putting a margin" around what "they say." In the same way that text on a page is laid out with white space and margins to allow for easier reading, I put a "margin" around what others tell me if I am being told something is impossible. This "margin" gives me some room in which to hold the possibility that there is another way to look at the situation and that the "experts" could, in fact, be wrong. Very wrong.

That was the case of the fund-raising experts my ministry hired to launch a capital campaign to raise money to buy our own building. We needed to raise $500,000 in cash within six months and secure a $1.4 million loan. The consultants interviewed our members and analyzed our demographics. I can still remember the moment when I got the results. It was a Sunday morning right before my first service. The fax line rang and in came their report. Though my inner guidance told me to wait to read it, my curiosity got the better of me and I nervously yanked the paper from the fax machine. Buried within their explanations was their final analysis and expert opinion: *Your congregation will not support a $500,000 capital campaign. You can expect to raise no more than $19,000 in cash over the next six months.* Without the $500,000 in cash, we knew we wouldn't qualify for the $1.4 million loan we needed. By the way, we had paid these consultants $12,000!

My younger brother was visiting me at the time and saw the look of devastation on my face and the tears in my eyes as I finished reading. When I explained what the paper said, he took it from my hands, tore it in half and said: "Wendy, this is just a piece of paper with writing on it. Let's get another piece of paper and write something else on it instead." He was certainly challenging me to consider that "they could be wrong." And, in fact, they were. We did raise the $500,000 in cash we needed through a combination of gifts and promissory notes; we got our $1.4 million loan; we purchased our building; and we even paid off the mortgage and promissory notes well ahead of schedule!

> If an expert says it can't be done, get another expert.
> —David Ben-Gurion, Statesman

In order to tap into our inner genius, we need to suspend the doubts and limiting opinions of others while holding firmly to the knowledge that another way exists. When we embrace the potential for something larger and greater, our mind is irreversibly opened to new possibilities.

Ask Yourself *This*

Are my obstacles real or imagined?

For fun, Boy Scouts sometimes play games to initiate new members into their troop. In one such game, the scouts set up an obstacle course with chairs and explain to the new members that whoever makes it through the maze of chairs first wins. However, they have to make it through the obstacle course blindfolded. The contestants are given 30 seconds to study the layout of the obstacles before the blindfolds are put on. Then they are turned around three times. While this is happening, the rest of the troop quickly and quietly removes all the chairs. At the sound of the whistle the fun begins. The blindfolded scouts cautiously pick their way around and through a maze of obstacles that no longer exist.

How about you? Are your obstacles real or imagined? If they are in fact real, are they as big as you are making them? It's not healthy to deny our problems, but it is healthy—and wise—to question whether our fear is making them larger or more numerous. When we are willing to challenge ourselves and question how real our obstacles are, we may very likely find that they do not exist at all—or they may shrink through careful scrutiny and reveal themselves as true opportunities to unleash our inner genius.

Chapter Seven

Ask Yourself *This*

To Be More Successful

Most often, we view success as an external measurement of accomplishment. To feel successful, we want to manifest dramatic and visible changes. But success begins in the mind. Success starts as a mental shift in perspective and changing the way we look at life. Our wildest goals and dreams are simply latent possibilities waiting for us to realize their achievement is possible. Much of the process of becoming successful involves expanding your capacity to believe in what's possible.

In a culture more interested in the trappings of success, quick fixes and simple answers, we can easily become discouraged if our progress seems too slow or our results fall short of the media's picture of success. We can quickly fall into self-sabotaging patterns of thought and behavior that undermine our efforts. Rather than acting from an awareness of possibility and striving to succeed, we often struggle in doubt, simply trying to survive. Yet, in the words of Henry David Thoreau, "Men are born to succeed—not to fail."

> Self-trust is the first secret of success.
> —Ralph Waldo Emerson

> What we can or cannot do, what we consider possible or impossible, is rarely a function or our true capability. It is more likely a function of our beliefs about who we are.
> —Anthony Robbins, Author

It is the vision of who we want to become, the life we want to live, and the world we hope to bring forth that fires

> Some people change ...
> when they see the light; others when they feel the heat.
> —Caroline Schoeder

> The pain pushes until
> the vision pulls.
> —Rev. Dr. Michael Bernard Beckwith

our imagination and feeds our souls. While Caroline Schoeder and Rev. Michael Bernard Beckwith are absolutely right that some people are only motivated to change or grow as a result of negative circumstances, the questions in this chapter will help you move from being provoked by pain (or heat!) to being drawn forward by the brilliant vision of your highest, most successful life. These questions will help widen your perspective and move you from thoughts of doubt to ones of possibility.

Ask Yourself *This*

Is it really impossible?

This is one of my favorite questions. It forces me to acknowledge my often self-imposed limits and excuses and look far beyond them. Success is only possible when we look beyond limits and "impossibilities." Before the Wright brothers' first flight at Kitty Hawk in 1903, the limits of technology restricted humanity's movement to ground travel. But the Wright brothers

> The Difficult is that which can be done immediately; the Impossible, that which takes a little longer.
> —George Santayana, Philosopher

> It always seems impossible until it is done.
> —Nelson Mandela

didn't let this limitation stop them. They were determined to find a way, and, of course, they did. Limits and impossibilities are simply the result of prior failings—unsuccessful attempts we have adopted as absolute.

I am reminded of an inspiring story about an undergraduate student at the University of California-Berkeley named George Dantzig. One day George arrived late for his statistics class. He was greeted with two very difficult problems on the blackboard. Believing them to be homework, he copied them down and worked diligently on them for quite some time. After several days and much hard mental work, Dantzig gave his answers to his professor. About six weeks later, his professor came to his student's little apartment carrying a manuscript with him. He told Dantzig that the two problems on the blackboard were meant to be examples of problems that were impossible to solve. Yet Dantzig had solved them! The manuscript was Dantzig's work, ready to be published. Dantzig later became nicknamed the father of linear programming and taught mathematics at Stanford for more than three decades.[1]

What have you written on the blackboard of your life as unsolvable? Are you absolutely positive it is impossible? Remember, "impossible" is only a conclusion based on past failings. What would happen if you approached your problems without first labeling them impossible? What would you succeed in doing? You may not currently know the solution, but that does not mean one doesn't exist.

To help you stay open to possibility and allow for your greatest success, it is important to keep your mind open and flexible. Here are two simple practices that will help you stretch your mind and generate mental receptivity. The first

> In the beginner's mind there are many possibilities; in the expert's mind there are few.
> —Shunryu Suzuki, Japanese Statesman

> Don't wait until everything is just right. It will never be perfect. There will always be challenges, obstacles and less-than-perfect conditions. So what? Get started now. With each step you take, you will grow stronger and stronger, more and more skilled, more and more self-confident, and more and more successful.
> —Mark Victor Hansen, Author

is to practice sitting quietly for five to 10 minutes each day and imagine yourself holding the place of possibility. Suspend your doubts if only for these few minutes. You can always pick your doubt back up again, but for these five to 10 minutes allow yourself to breathe deeply and just wonder, "Is this really impossible?" Feel the edges, the boundaries of your mind dissolving as you move into the realm of free, limitless possibility thinking. Remind yourself not to assume it can't be done simply because it hasn't yet been done. Who knows what you may achieve that was previously labeled impossible?

This second practice is a playful one that at first glance appears contradictory to what I've previously written. However, it is very effective in expanding your capacity for creativity and imagination. It comes from Lewis Carroll's *Alice in Wonderland*. The Queen is criticizing Alice's rigid and too-literal thinking and challenges her: "When I was your age, I always believed in impossible things. Why, sometimes I've believed as many as six impossible things before breakfast." The practice, then, is to spend a few minutes every day believing six "impossible" but really exciting things you'd like to bring into your life. Be as creative and outrageous as you want. Not only is this practice fun, but you may be surprised when you look back upon these lists several months or years from now at how some of those impossible things have actually come to pass.

> Nothing is impossible; there are ways that lead to everything, and if we had sufficient will we should always have sufficient means. It is often merely for an excuse that we say things are impossible.
>
> —François de la Rochefoucauld, Writer

Let me share one personal example of the power of this exercise. For many months I had been practicing believing that something totally amazing would happen that would put Unity and The Unity Center (where I serve) on the map. I had no idea what that might be. It was just fun to believe and feel that it would happen. About six months later, I was presented with the opportunity to be Unity's "Oprah" and interview Dr. Deepak Chopra on his new book *The Third Jesus: The Christ We Cannot Ignore*, for a six-part Webinar series done in the fashion of Oprah's highly successful Webinar with Eckhart Tolle on *A New Earth*. A producer, coach and television crew were brought to San Diego to film the conversations before a live audience at The Unity Center. It was magical! We called the series *Jesus and The Awakening to God-Consciousness,* and nearly 12,000 viewers watched it on Unity.FM (Unity's online radio network).

But that's not all! The conversations were so rich and the quality so high, that both Deepak Chopra and Bruce Marcus, the producer, felt the programs should be shown on public television. KQED, the public broadcasting station in San Francisco, with more than 1.5 million households viewing per month, was approached and agreed to broadcast the programs and test-market them. The programs did quite well! And plans are currently under way to syndicate the program in many of the major public broadcasting markets across the county, I'd say that has the potential to put Unity and The Unity Center "on the map," wouldn't you?

Ask Yourself *This*

If I could solve the "how," what would I do?

This question presents a powerful concept that I first heard from a church-growth consultant named Howard Kelly. Our ministry hired Howard because we were growing rapidly. We had outgrown our facility and needed to lease additional space so we could double the capacity of our sanctuary. But when it came time to expand the sanctuary, we realized we would have to change the room's orientation and reverse the location of the stage. The new placement of the stage would necessitate relocating the sanctuary's main entrance doors. This presented a problem. There were only two viable options where the new doors could be placed: one that was clearly the correct and more functional option but which also happened to be more expensive and difficult, and another that was much easier and less expensive but compromised functionality.

When Howard and I discussed the placement of the doors, he kept advocating for the better, more functional option despite the fact it was more difficult to achieve structurally and financially. I, on the other hand, argued that we didn't have the money or resources for the better option. I presented a rather compelling list of all the problems that prevented the better option from being feasible. Howard listened patiently and then simply but firmly said, "Wendy, you've got to separate problem-solving from decision-making. If you could solve the problems, where would you put the doors?" That was not what I wanted to hear, and my first fleeting thought was to smack him (despite being committed to nonviolence and having never even spanked my children) because it was so obvious what the right answer was when I asked the right question! There was no doubt where the doors needed to be.

His question forced me to separate problem-solving from decision-making and gave me a new (and better) perspective. Did the issues and problems still exist? Absolutely, but I didn't allow them to interfere with what I knew was the right choice. Sure enough, we were able to solve the problems and put the doors where they needed to be. But if I hadn't asked myself the question Howard suggested, I would have opted for the easier, less expensive solution with a much less desirable result.

I've also applied this practice with other important personal decisions—including whether to have children! While taking a walk one morning, I found myself thinking about my biological clock and realizing that if I was going to have children, I'd better not wait much longer. (I was about thirty-four at the time.) The idea of motherhood both thrilled and frightened me. How in the world could I possibly do it all? How could I be the kind of mother I wanted to be while still serving as the minister of a large and growing church with the many responsibilities and demands on my time that entailed? The more I thought about it, the more I got stuck in trying to figure out the "how." The more I got stuck in trying to figure out the "how," the further I got from what really mattered to me. It took me awhile to realize that I was, once again, starting at the wrong place: I was asking the wrong question. In a flash, Howard Kelly's voice popped into my head and, though this time in an entirely different context, I heard his words: "If you could solve the problems, what would your decision be?" In that instant, without any doubt whatsoever, I had my answer. I knew what I wanted—and though I still didn't know "how" I was going to balance everything, I had the clarity, confidence and energy to know that I (along with my husband, of course) would be able to figure it out. I practically ran home to share the good news with my husband John! We are now the very happy and proud parents of two beautiful children—Johnathon, who is about to enter college, and Jennifer, who is completing middle school. Not only did I figure out how to do motherhood and ministry, I also figured out how to homeschool our children. (But that's another story.)

Considering the many challenges facing our world today—global warming, hunger, poverty, pandemic disease—this is a particularly timely question for all of us to consider: "If I could solve the 'how,' what would I do?" Now, more than ever, we must base our decisions on what is in the highest and best interest of all sentient beings as well as our planet itself—not merely what is easiest, quickest or least expensive. Only when we separate problem-solving from decision-making will we make the quality of decisions needed to move beyond our current challenges to build a better world.

Ask Yourself *This*

"If I knew I would be successful, what would I be saying 'yes' to?"

Stop reading right now. Take a deep breath. Close your eyes and consider this question deeply: If you knew you would succeed, what would you be saying "yes" to? Are there any differences between your answer and the way you are living your life today? The very nature of this question invites you to step beyond the size of the life you've known until now.

I am reminded of a story my Unity minister of many years ago, Rev. Robert Stevens, told. A man was happily fishing for trout in a beautiful mountain stream. He was doing very well and catching a lot of fish. Every time he caught a fish, he'd take out his ruler and measure what he had caught. Sometimes he'd keep the fish and put it on his stringer. Other times, he'd throw what he caught back in the stream. Another man noticed he was doing something very odd—it seemed he was keeping the small fish and throwing the big ones away! Watching him do this with almost a dozen fish, the onlooker couldn't control his curiosity any longer.

Approaching him, the onlooker asked, "What are you doing? I notice you keep measuring the fish and throwing the bigger ones back. Why?"

"Oh, that's simple! I measure the fish to see if it's nine inches or less. If it's less than nine inches I keep it. If it's more than nine inches I throw it away," he answered.

"But why?" the onlooker persisted.

"Because I only have a nine-inch frying pan at home!"

Spirit, God, Universal Mind—whatever you want to call the Ineffable Presence—wants you to catch *and keep* the big fish! But you're going to have to have a large enough frying pan. You're going to have to be willing to increase your capacity. Many people don't, though, because even if their current life is not what they want, it feels safe, comfortable, familiar and secure. It requires no change; no risk. So, they consciously—or unconsciously—throw the big fish back in the stream.

A question like this invites us to leave behind what we have always known and step into the vision we have held—however secretly and however long—for the greatest possibility for our life. What dreams lie dormant within you because you have feared you would fail? What is the worst that could happen if you let those dreams take flight? Or a more fitting question might be "What is the *best* that could happen?" Will there be risk involved? Yes, but success never comes without risk. Will you progress in a straight and predictable line? Probably not. But, as Susan Scott writes in *Fierce Conversations*, "Life is curly; don't try to straighten it out."[2] Will you have all the answers when you begin? Unlikely, but you are armed with the right questions to attract the answers you need. Be rigorously honest with yourself. Ask yourself, "How long am I going to put this off and how much of me will die if I don't act on it?"

> The first step toward success is taken when you refuse to be a captive of the environment in which you first find yourself.
> —Mark Caine, Author

> For true success ask yourself these four questions: Why? Why not? Why not me? Why not now?
> —James Allen, Author

Despite the rather daunting prospect of going after our dreams, none of the risks compares with the price we pay for not pursuing them. And, if we still find it a bit difficult to muster the courage, perhaps it will help to realize that the world needs exactly what we are secretly dreaming of giving and becoming.

Ask Yourself *This*

Who do I need to become to manifest what I want?

Whenever I am working on a personal or professional goal, I ask myself this question because it deals with who we are at the very deepest level and how we show up in the world. Thinking about what you want in life, the kind of work you want to do, the kind of relationships you want to have, and the kind of world you want to live in is important. Setting goals is important. So is the practice of visualization and affirmation. But the question "Who must I become?" is at the heart of achieving any personal or professional goal.

> Listen to life, and you will hear the voice of life crying, Be!
> —James Dillet Freeman

> It is not enough to be busy; so are the ants. The question is: What are we busy about?
> —Henry David Thoreau

We can practice a level of *being* that embodies the key characteristics required to meet our goals. Perhaps it's creativity. Compassion. Confidence. Courage. Maybe we need to be bold. Daring. Adventuresome. Outgoing.

We often think of success as achieving the goal. But just as important, if not more important, is how we grow and change as we pursue the goal. While the significance of reaching a goal may fade with time, who we had to become in order to reach it is eternal. The recent economic crises have shown us just how temporary much of what we accumulate or build in the outer can be. But who we have become can never be taken from us, regardless of circumstances.

Ask Yourself *This*

What can I do next?

Asking ourselves this simple question can help immeasurably when we feel overwhelmed and overburdened. Perhaps what is most challenging today is the sheer number of responsibilities we all face each day. Trying to deal with them all at once is overwhelming and impractical. So ask yourself the simple question "What can I do next?"

In our backyard we have two lovely, prolific peach trees. Toward the end of San Diego's mild winters, these trees produce an abundance of blossoms that will become fruit. In the early spring, when the blossoms yield to the small fruit, I'm faced with the difficult task of thinning the fruit. It's not the physical work that is difficult; it's some resistance in me to reducing the abundance. Yet I know that if I don't thin the tree, and leave all of the fruit to mature, every peach will be very small. The only way the tree will produce large, lush, sweet peaches is if I thin it.

> We say we waste time, but that is impossible. We waste ourselves.
> —Alice Bloch, Author

> The only reason for time is so that everything doesn't happen at once.
> —Albert Einstein

Just as my peach trees can't nurture all their blossoms into large, succulent fruit, we cannot say yes to every choice and possibility in our lives and be truly successful. We have to choose.

Where do you need to do some pruning in your life? Where do you need to cut back or postpone in order to give your energy to what is most important? What do you need to release? What do you need to stop doing altogether?

Selecting what is yours to do is important, and choosing

what is yours to do *now* is essential. Each of us has unique passions, interests, skills and opportunities to cultivate specific talents. We are not meant to do everything, nor can we.

Ask yourself, "What can I do next?" and then allow Spirit to guide you in the right direction.

When I was a teenager, I told my grandmother that I wanted to live to be 120 years old. She wanted to know why. My answer was, "There is too much to do! There are so many things that sound interesting to me. I can't possibly do them all if I only live to be 70. So I want to live to be 120! That should give me enough time."

Though I still plan to live a long time, I have come to appreciate the deep wisdom of choosing a few dreams, projects or goals and then fully devoting my energy to them. Notice that while we have two hands, two eyes, two ears and two legs, we have but one heart and one mind to our purpose. Find what is yours to do and then go for it!

> Your time is limited, so don't waste it living someone else's life. Don't be trapped by dogma—which is living with the results of other people's thinking. Don't let the noise of others' opinions drown out your own inner voice. And most important, have the courage to follow your heart and intuition. They somehow already know what you truly want to become.
> —Steve Jobs, Business Leader

Ask Yourself *This*

What greater good is wanting to come forth?

Everything happens for a reason. We may not know the reason at the time, but one ending becomes another beginning. For every door that closes, another opens. Such a promise can give us hope and encouragement if we experience "a dark night of the soul."

The question, "What greater good is wanting to come forth?" redirects our attention from negativity and fear to openness and possibility. We would be wise to remember the adage, "When one door closes, another one opens." We have to stop looking at the closed door in order to see the open one.

Though we long for the right answer, it is often the right question at the right time that we need *first*. That question will redirect our attention and open us to another level of energy and support, a *spiritual* level of energy and support. Success is being able to view adversity as an opportunity to demonstrate strength and resiliency. Consider challenge to be like sandpaper to your soul. Though it is rough and uncomfortable, it results in a smoother, more polished and refined you.

The question "What greater good is wanting to come forth?" helps us view current situations with great hope and optimism. In addition, this question reminds us that there is no place where

> I will prepare and some day my chance will come.
> —Abraham Lincoln
>
> For everything you have missed, you have gained something.
> —Ralph Waldo Emerson

Spirit is not! Even in the darkest, most frightening times and situations when we feel most alone, there *is* a greater Presence and Power available to us. It is not missing; we have simply fallen asleep to it. We sometimes think it's hard to find God, when in reality it is impossible to *avoid* God. God, Spirit, is everywhere, equally present and accessible at all times. It is we who sometimes forget this.

Sincerely asking this question cannot help but change our thoughts and perspective and, therefore, our experiences. Success is not measured by our ability to prevent hardship; it is measured by the way we perceive and respond to difficulty. Such challenges may even lead to success beyond our wildest dreams.

Chapter Eight

Ask Yourself *This*

To Practice at Home

Bedtime was always a special time for me with my children. It gave me very special private time with each of them in which I could fully enter into their worlds.

Though I love my work and am deeply committed to it, being the very best mother I can be has always been my top priority. I know that all the things we wish to see happen in the world must first happen within ourselves and within our families or they will never happen in the world at all.

In his poem "The Hand That Rocks the Cradle," William Ross Wallace reminds us:

Blessings on the hand of women!
Angels guard its strength and grace,
In the palace, cottage, hovel,
Oh, no matter where the place;
Would that never storms assailed it,
Rainbows ever gently curled;
For the hand that rocks the cradle
Is the hand that rules the world.

Infancy's the tender fountain,
Power may with beauty flow,
Mother's first to guide the streamlets,
From them souls unresting grow—
Grow on for the good or evil,
Sunshine streamed or evil hurled;
For the hand that rocks the cradle
Is the hand that rules the world.[1]

In the sixth century B.C.E., philosopher Lao Tse wrote, "If there is peace in the heart, there will be beauty in the character. If there is beauty in the character, there will be harmony in the home. If there is harmony in the home, there will be order in the nation. When there is order in the nation, there will be peace in the world."

As you may recall, in chapter seven I wrote about how I applied the teaching, "If you could solve the problems, what would your decision be?" into my decision to become a mother. That same process eventually led to the decision my husband, John, and I made to homeschool our children. That was no small task, since both of us work full-time for The Unity Center and neither of us is a formal educator. But when we considered our values as a family, our deep desire for our children to not only be well-educated but also to retain a lifelong curiosity and love of learning, and our desire to help them to grow into conscious global citizens, we found ourselves seriously doubting whether these goals could be met within the current structure of public education. So when it was time for Johnathon to enter kindergarten, we decided to opt for homeschooling. That began a journey that continues to this day and includes our daughter Jennifer. (It is important for me to add here that despite the fact that I am a minister, our decision to homeschool was not at all a religious one. In fact, I do not consider myself to be religious. I am, however, deeply spiritual.)

> To understand your parents' love, you must raise children yourself.
> —Chinese Proverb

> Making the decision to have a child—it's momentous. It is to decide forever to have your heart walking around outside your body.
> —Elizabeth Stone, Author

Did we have it all figured out in the beginning? Absolutely not. But we knew what was important to us and why it was important. Plus, we knew there wasn't anything our children needed to learn in their first few years of school that we couldn't teach them. Over the years their schooling has changed from pure home-schooling to participating in an outstanding virtual charter school (California Virtual Academies). However, they still do not attend a brick-and-mortar school. They still come with us every day (as they have since they were babies) to The Unity Center, where we work and where they have their own office to do their studies. Though we continue to be directly involved in their education, they now have access to a whole team of credentialed teachers and study one of the most robust curricula in the nation, including courses in foreign languages and advanced placement courses for college. (I cannot recommend this program highly enough for parents who want their children to receive an outstanding education and also want to remain the primary influence in their children's lives when it comes to values.)

> Education is not the filling of a pail, but the lighting of a fire.
> —W. B. Yeats
>
> You cannot teach a man anything; you can only help him find it within himself.
> —Galileo

This is how Johnathon explained his educational background on his recent college admissions application:

I never experienced that exciting and yet deathly terrifying first day of kindergarten. Because I was homeschooled, all I did was wander into my mom's office, plop down in a chair, and begin. The only reason I had to let go of her hand was to hold the pencil. My entire life I have learned through unconventional means, which has offered a few challenges but many once-in-a-lifetime opportunities.

Though my school lacks a football team, a mascot and even a building, I feel great pride in saying I attend California Virtual Academies (CAVA). In many respects, CAVA functions like a traditional high school. I have certified teachers for all my classes and must adhere to deadlines just like any other student. I take tests and am awarded grades. The difference is it is all online. Since the Internet belongs to no district, my classmates are scattered throughout California which makes it impossible to have clubs, bands and team sports. However, for everything CAVA has not been able to give, it has provided me with opportunities I feel are even more valuable. As long as I adhere to assignment deadlines, I can create my schedule ... This flexibility has allowed me to travel the globe and meet world leaders such as the Dalai Lama and Ela Gandhi (Mahatma Gandhi's granddaughter).

Though I have never set foot in a public school and been able to call myself a student there, my feet have wandered the world. Despite never having seen the homecoming game, I have played soccer with Malawian children who would rival even the most professional athletes. I am not an average student because I don't come from an average school. I am different, but I don't view my dissimilarity as a weakness; I see it as my greatest strength.

There's a reason I've taken some time to share this more personal material. During so much of the 13-year journey of providing a nontraditional form of education for my children while maintaining a career, I have had to practice being sure I was asking the right questions along the way. I've also had to get comfortable accepting that some questions couldn't be or didn't need to be answered right away.

When John and I decided to homeschool our children (and as a natural result create a very unique work and family lifestyle), we not only had plenty of questions ourselves, but because of my public profile we also had a lot of questions posed to us by others. Well-meaning neighbors, friends, colleagues and congregants would ask us questions like, "What are you going to do about senior prom?" "What about extracurricular activities?" "How about sports?" "How are you going to teach calculus or science?" "What about getting in to college?" And the ubiquitous, "What about socialization? Aren't you worried that your kids are going to grow up socially inept or not have any friends?"

Most of these would be legitimate questions that we would eventually need to answer. But we started getting these types of questions when Johnathon was only in first grade! We certainly didn't have all these answers then. It took us a little while, and a little more maturing, to realize we didn't need to answer all those questions at the very beginning. That in itself was a very important lesson and a growth opportunity for us. We held the questions—the good and important ones—and eventually really great answers came. Through California Virtual Academies all the academic and college preparation questions were answered. As for those questions about sports: Johnathon has been a student of the martial art of aikido since he was 12 and is currently training for his black belt. He has also become an expert downhill skier. He's attended numerous dances with his girlfriend, who attends a traditional high school, and took her to her senior prom.

As for socialization and extracurricular activities, I'll let him speak for himself one more time.

> By my senior year, I had been to 15 different countries; spoken at the United Nations on the necessity of global cooperation; and built two schools in rural Africa. From this global exposure I realized how similar we all are. As a 13-year-old speaking before 500 other teens at the United Nations, I knew there is no age requirement for making a difference in the world. In addition, spearheading

the fund-raising of $33,000 to fund a school in Africa and participating in its construction showed me nothing is impossible when we work together. These experiences reinforced my belief that though we are whole as individuals, we are all part of a greater totality that transcends the pieces that comprise it. In short, each individual on this planet is a member of the larger human family, and as metaphoric family members it is our responsibility to help one another. It is my wish to fully live out the advice the Dalai Lama once gave me. When I asked him what I could do to change the world, he paused and said, "Study ... and love everyone as your mother has loved you."

As for college, as of this writing, Johnathon's been accepted into several prominent universities, including University of California-Berkeley.

As I have emphasized throughout this book, asking the right questions *first* is very important, but *so is knowing which questions need to be answered when.* Not every good question has to be answered at the beginning of the journey. Some are best answered along the way.

Three Questions

While we try to teach our children all about life, our children teach us what life is all about.
    —Angela Schwindt, Author

A happy family is but an earlier heaven.
—George Bernard Shaw, Author

I'm not exactly sure how it started, but when Johnathon was about six or seven years old, I started to use our bedtime routine as a time to check into his little world more deeply. It probably began with my asking him the usual and rather empty question, "How was your day?" Finding that it often elicited little more than "Good" or "Okay," I decided to come up with some better questions.

And so each evening as I would tuck him into bed, I would ask "What happened today that made you feel happy inside?" Then I would listen with my full attention. When he would finish I'd ask, "Was there anything that happened today that made you feel sad?" (Of course, if the answer was "yes," I would probe deeper and say, "Tell me about that.") I'd listen again and then ask a third question. "Is there anything about today that you wish had been different?" And of course, I'd listen again.

From time to time, I would substitute different feelings for the first two inquiries. For the first question I might ask, "What happened today that made you feel proud? (or loved, brave, strong, smart?)" For the second question I might ask, "Was there anything that happened today that made you feel angry?" (or afraid, embarrassed, ashamed, confused, unloved, disliked?)" The third question might become, "Is there anything that happened today that you wish you could have changed?"

> There is no doubt that it is around the family and the home that all the greatest virtues, the most dominating virtues of human society are created, strengthened and maintained.
> —Winston Churchill

> Every father should remember that one day his son will follow his example instead of his advice.
> —Unknown

Soon John was having his own special one-on-one time asking Johnathon the questions. (Afterwards, we would sometimes compare the answers we received.) As soon as our daughter Jennifer was old enough, we started the same routine with her. Our bedtime routine definitely got longer, but our relationships grew sweeter and deeper.

As the children grew older, our questions became more thought-provoking. Rather than asking what made them happy, we'd ask, "What did you appreciate today?" That was usually followed by something like, "What challenged you today?" or "Where did you have to stretch or grow today?"

The third question changed the most and in many ways became the most valuable. It's one that I believe, if sincerely asked by every parent to his or her preteen on a regular basis, would go a long, long way in keeping that relationship healthy and strong during those years when it is most vulnerable to being threatened and damaged by negative influences.

As the opportunities and responsibilities of my work expanded, I began feeling some parental guilt as a career mom. Despite having my children with me at work every day and juggling my part of the homeschooling responsibilities during my long lunch hour, I wondered if I was doing a good enough job as a mother. Did my children really feel like I was there for them? Was I an "askable" parent? Could they, would they, come to me with what might be on their minds?

Those questions percolated in my mind for a few weeks. Then one evening I found myself asking Johnathon, "Is there anything you've been wanting to talk to me about that you didn't know how to bring up or that you thought I might have been too busy to hear?"

That question has opened the door to some of the richest, deepest and most important conversations I've had with my children. It helped to create a very special, sacred and dependable safe space for them to share anything from questions about first crushes and falling in love to hopes and fears about growing up. Even in very close families, it can be difficult for children to bring up certain things that are on their minds and in their hearts, especially if the topics are awkward or embarrassing or if the children feel their parents are too busy. A question like this one, when asked regularly, builds in a natural and easy time for them to open up.

Over the years as a result of this simple bedtime practice, our children have learned to identify their feelings, recognize their blessings, speak confidently about what's on their minds and be more thoughtful and introspective. As parents, we have experienced the privilege of entering more fully into the precious and magical world of their childhood before it is gone.

In closing, I hope the simple yet deep wisdom expressed in *If a Child* inspires you in how you approach the children you come in contact with—whether your own or not—as it has inspired me.

If a Child
If a child lives with Criticism,
He learns to Condemn.
If a child lives with Hostility,
He learns to Fight.

If a child lives with Ridicule,
He learns to be Shy.
If a child lives with Shame,
He learns to feel Guilty.

If a child lives with Tolerance,
He learns to be Patient.
If a child lives with Encouragement,
He learns Confidence.

If a child lives with Praise,
He learns to Appreciate.

If a child lives with Fairness,
He learns Justice.
If a child lives with Security,
He learns to have Faith.

If a child lives with Approval,
He learns to Like Himself.

If a child lives with Acceptance and Friendship,
He learns to find Love in the World.

—Author Unknown

Notes

Introduction

1. Michael Schulman, "Great Minds Start With Great Questions," *Parents* Magazine, September 1993.

Chapter One

1. George H. Gallup Jr., "American's Spiritual Searches Turn Inward," February 13, 2003. *Gallup.com*, 2009. <http://www.gallup.com/poll/7759/Americans-Spiritual-Searches-Turn-Inward.aspx>.

2. Martha Smock, "No Other Way," *Daily Word*, Unity Village, Missouri: Silent Unity, 1947.

3. Sharon Begley, "Science Finds God," *Newsweek*, July 20, 1998.

4. Edwin Markham, "Outwitted," *The Shoes of Happiness and Other Poems*, Garden City, New York: Doubleday, Page and Co., 1915.

5. "The First Suspension Bridge," *Niagara Falls Thunder Alley*, June 13, 2009. Ed. Rick Berketa. June 17, 2009 <http://www.niagarafrontier.com/bridges.html#b2>.

Chapter Two

1. Marianne Williamson, *A Return to Love*, HarperCollins, 1996.

Chapter Three

No notes for Chapter Three.

Chapter Four

1. Ingrid Bengis, *Combat in the Erogenous Zone*, New York: Knopf (Distributed by Random House), 1972.

2. Og Mandino, *A Better Way to Live*, Bantam Books, 1990.

3. Glenn Clark, *The Man Who Tapped the Secrets of the Universe*, The University of Science and Philosophy, 1946.

4. Ibid.

5. May Rowland, *Dare to Believe*, Unity Village, Missouri: Unity House, 1961.

Chapter Five

1. Gene Weingarten, "Pearls Before Breakfast," *The Washington Post*, April 8, 2007.

2. Ibid.

3. Ken Keyes Jr., *Prescriptions for Happiness*, Love Line Books, 1981.

4. Monsignor Jim Lisante, *Western Catholic Reporter*, <http//www.msgrlisante.org/archived_message. asp?ID=170> August 9, 2006.

5. Ibid.

Chapter Six

1. Friedrich Gauss story, September 15, 2002. June 17, 2009. <http://www.newton.dep.anl.gov/askasci/math99/math99155.htm>

2. Don Miguel Ruiz, *The Four Agreements*, Amber-Allen Publishing, 1997.

3. Ibid.

Chapter Seven

1. Jeremy Pearce, "George B. Dantzig Dies at 90," *The New York Times*, May 23, 2005.

2. Susan Scott, *Fierce Conversations*, New York: Berkley Publishing, 2002.

Chapter Eight

1. William Ross Wallace, "The Hand That Rocks the Cradle," *Poems That Live Forever*, by Hazel Felleman, Doubleday, 1965.

Acknowledgements

To: Charlotte Shelton, president and CEO of Unity School of Christianity, for your friendship, support and belief in this book; Paula Coppel, vice president of communications for Unity, for your trust and the opportunity to play "Oprah" interviewing Dr. Deepak Chopra for *Jesus and the Awakening to God-Consciousness;* Mindy Audlin, producer for Unity.FM; Le Grande Greene, media coach, for your very strong push to get this book out there fast; and Stephanie Oliver, editorial director of Unity House Books, for making it happen.

To: My special friends and cheerleaders: Cindy Henson, Dana Smith, Mark Weaver, John McNeil and Christine Elliott; my true soul sister, Barbara Fields; and Jeanne and Karl Anthony, two of my favorite people on the planet, for all your personal love and support.

To: Savella Davidson for years of volunteer service and Janet Poser for being our full-time "volunteer" at The Unity Center; we could not do what we do without you! To Judy Bennett, for making me promise to stay in San Diego; Barbara Masters for making me look and feel good; Brian O'Neil, for seeing in me qualities I sometimes have a hard time seeing and for letting me be your "sistuh!" and to Mary Holladay for finding that missing tape.

To some of my many teachers along the way: Dr. Wayne Dyer, Deepak Chopra, Marianne Williamson, Barbara Marx Hubbard, James Newton, Rev. Michael Bernard Beckwith, Ecknath Easwaran, Wayne Muller, Eckhart Tolle, Byron Katie and Rev. Robert Stevens, my first Unity minister.

To: My brother, Bill, for catapulting me on the personal growth path when you gave me Wayne Dyer's book *Your Erroneous Zones* and for tearing up that fax from the fundraising experts.

To: My sister, Lorra, for her love and dedication to me and The Unity Center for more than 13 years.

To: The Board of Advisors and staff of The Unity Center and to all those—past and present—who have been a part of this great spiritual community. You have enriched my life and the world immensely.

About the Author

Wendy Craig-Purcell is founding minister and CEO of The Unity Center, a 1500-member spiritual community in San Diego, California. The Unity Center, formerly known as Church of Today, celebrated its 25-year anniversary in May 2008. Wendy is a graduate of the Unity School of Christianity, Unity Village, Missouri. She was ordained in 1980, one of the youngest ministers to ever be ordained in Unity.

Wendy has been active for many years in the Association for Global New Thought (AGNT). She joined its Leadership Council in 1999 and currently serves as vice president. Wendy participated in all three AGNT-sponsored "Synthesis Dialogues," which brought together some of the world's leading thinkers to dialogue with His Holiness the Dalai Lama. The dialogues were held in Dharmsala, India, in 1999 and in Italy in 2001 and 2004.

Wendy has been involved with other important AGNT activities, including producing six large-scale "Awakened World" conferences and the Gandhi King Peace Train and Living Legends of Nonviolence Conference. She traveled to Istanbul, Turkey, in November 2006 as part of the planning for the Abraham Path Initiative, in partnership with the Harvard Negotiation Project, to open a pilgrimage route in the Middle East retracing the footsteps of the prophet Abraham.

Wendy has been active in a variety of other Unity and New Thought organizations. She has served as president and treasurer of the Southwest Unity Region; as district president of the International New Thought Alliance; and as chairman of the Association of Unity Churches International Church Growth Committee.

In addition, Wendy serves on the board of the Foundation for Affordable Housing in San Juan Capistrano. Her service awards include the Gandhi Nonviolence Award from the Tariq Khamisa Foundation and induction into the Martin

Luther King Jr. Board of Preachers Hall of Fame.

With a strong interest in spiritually motivated social action, Wendy and The Unity Center were instrumental in the early formation of the San Diego Department of Peace grassroots group in the fall of 2004. That initial group, Americans for the Department of Peace, now encompasses all of Southern California, with The Unity Center providing ongoing support.

Wendy lives in San Diego, California (Scripps Ranch), with her husband, John Purcell, who serves as director of operations for The Unity Center, and their two children, Johnathon and Jennifer.

B0080